Evangeline

A Story of Faith

BY BETTE NORDBERG

Dedication

To: David Jeremiah, who said,
"Be ready to take the hill country."

And to Cheryl, who said,
"You can do it."

And to Jill Jaquard, who spent endless
hours proofing, so that I could finish.

Many Thanks.

Preface

This story is largely the result of interviews and information gathered by Joe and Louise Nogel over five years. To present this information in a readable format, I have written in a novel-like style. Each story and the details surrounding it are taken directly from interviews. The conversations are quoted as nearly as possible from the memories of those involved. Mrs. Evangeline McNeill was an excellent writer, and many details are taken from her own written accounts of the stories. However, her own attempt to write the story of her life was left incomplete when she died in 1977. Some liberty has been taken in an attempt to "fill in" the feelings and actions of main characters. It is our hope that this recreation of her story is both accurate and readable, while at the same time compelling and inspiring. Mrs. Evangeline McNeill certainly had all of these characteristics.

Table of Contents

Chapter

The Author

Bette Nordberg, her husband, Kim, and their four children live in Puyallup, Washington. After graduating from the University of Washington in 1977 with a degree in Physical Therapy, Bette worked in rehabilitation medicine. After starting her family, the author turned her attention to writing and music. She has been extensively involved in Women's Ministries, teaching and writing Bible studies. She was part of a church planting team which began a new Saturday night church in Puyallup in 1991. Today, she writes and directs drama, and plays worship piano for Lighthouse Christian Center on South Hill, Puyallup.

Bette Nordberg

Bette Nordberg and her family first visited Cannon Beach Christian Conference Center in 1981. They have returned every summer since. In 1990, Bette volunteered to finish the writing of Mrs. McNeill's biography. It has been a five-year labor of love.

1

Summer's End

$\mathfrak{I}$t was a beautiful morning in early August. The sky over the ocean, was a clear, brilliant blue, uninterrupted by clouds. By the time breakfast was over, it was already hot. The radio reported temperatures expected to rise to 105 degrees F. in Portland, but as usual, ocean breezes would moderate temperatures at the coast. Guests at Cannon Beach Christian Conference Center (then known as Cannon Beach Bible Conference) found themselves eagerly anticipating a day of fun activities in extraordinary weather.

So far this week, things were going well. Evangeline Duff McNeill was proud of how far the conference center had come in only seven years. No longer did guests bring their ration books. No longer did the specter of war hover over their conferences. Still, in 1952, it was only a fledgling operation. But such hopes, such dreams she and her husband Archie shared for its growth. How grateful she was.

Archie's prediction was right. People from all over the northwest would head for the Oregon coast and this wonderful recreational setting to enjoy the best of the nation's Bible teachers. It was clear, even now, that God's hand was on all their plans. To her, it was a constant source of joy and excitement to watch Him miraculously provide for the needs of the conference center.

Evangeline knew that the conference center belonged to God. It was His project. But still, by virtue of their calling it became Archie and Evangeline's life blood. From the beginning, they had watched it grow. In prayer and in hard work, they had given birth to it, and guided it toward maturity.

This morning she was especially proud of Archie. People called him a real "platform man." And though they had been married for 16 years, she was always surprised by the way he managed a crowd. Even hosting breakfast is an art form to him, she mused. He was a giant of a man, six feet four inches, weighing nearly 260 pounds. But with a rich Scottish brogue, and a warm friendly manner, the guests of the center, strangers at first, found themselves part of a much larger family. Each week, Archie and Evangeline watched rich and lasting friendships develop. Believing in the importance and significance of each guest, they worked together to make all feel welcome— Archie from the platform, and Evangeline in her own personal, almost motherly way.

On this clear, warm morning, with breakfast over, and the guests dismissed, Archie moved quickly toward the table where Evangeline sat with her brother, Walter Duff, and his wife, Edith. "I'm headed into Portland now," he said, patting her hand.

"Don't you want me to come along?" she asked.

"No, you stay behind today, honey. It's too hot for you to sit in the car waiting for me ."

As she walked him toward the car, she asked again. "Are you sure Archie? I always come along." With a hug and kiss, he insisted she stay behind.

Cannon Beach was a small village on the North Oregon coast. Little in the way of restaurant supplies and groceries were locally available. As a result, a weekly trip to Portland was necessary during the summer. The conference center was always run with a skeleton crew, and Archie took the responsibility of these shopping trips. As Evangeline watched his car head on to the street, she felt uneasy about not going along.

As the day progressed, she found herself remembering other trips to Portland. She thought fondly of silent hours in the car holding hands. Were other couples able to spend hours enveloped in the same quiet world of love and understanding, she wondered.

Evangeline continued as usual through her daily tasks. She gave Isabelle, her oldest daughter, permission to take little Helen Jean on a walk to the beach. How wonderful that Isabelle loved caring for Helen Jean. Though they were 10 years apart, they enjoyed one another's company.

Through her day, Evangeline found her mind returning again and again to Archie's trip to Portland. He had always wanted her with him. Even when he was away for a speaking engagement, invariably he called late in the evening saying, "I just arrived in Portland. I'll be home as soon as I can." He hated to stay away from her when he was so close to home. No matter how late, or how Evangeline begged for him to spend the night in the city, he would head directly for the coast. In those days, the Sunset Highway, which led from Portland to the coast, was carved into the rugged coastal mountains. It was a tortuous drive, even for well-rested drivers in daylight hours. She spent many sleepless hours praying as she waited to hear his car turn on to the gravel driveway of the conference center.

Returning to the moment, she busied herself again with her guests and conference responsibilities.

It had been a long drive from Seattle, Washington, to Cannon Beach, Oregon. Bob and Sally McGrath arrived at the conference center with two children. They were all tired and hungry. Not knowing anything about the center's work , Bob had agreed to lead the worship portion of the services in exchange for room and board. It might not be much of a vacation, but it was free. Sally was full of dashed hopes as she climbed the stairs of the old log hotel. The upper floor was dark and unheated, and the walls between the rooms were made of boards riddled with open knotholes. The only evidence of the working stove downstairs were clouds of smoke in the upstairs hallway. The vacation might be free, she thought, but still the cost was too high. In spite of his disappointment in the facilities, Bob put his all into the services. As the week progressed, he and Sally found themselves irresistibly drawn to the spirit of the place and the graciousness of their host and hostess. There was no less smoke in the upstairs hallway, yet somehow, it seemed to matter less.

Tuesday, August 5, 1952 was a slow moving day. The station was full of the smell of perspiration and the sound of irritability. It is too hot to be on duty today, thought Pete. However, his sluggishness evaporated when he heard the radio calling his fire team to the Sunset highway accident. No matter how often he saw them, Pete never viewed the tragedy of a collision lightly. And as he came into view of this accident, the sick heavy feeling returned to his stomach. A large dump truck was turned onto its side on the wrong side of the highway. Lying across the road was a late model maroon sedan. Its front end was nearly nonexistent. Broken glass was everywhere. The driver was slumped over the steering wheel. Eggs and flour were strewn all over the hillside. Pete's crew split up immediately, some to help the driver of the truck, who seemed only slightly injured. Some went immediately to the car. Gently, they lifted the large middle-aged man onto the roadway. The medical team took over. Though the injured man was conscious, Pete's experienced eyes could see that he was badly hurt. Where was the ambulance?

By now, onlookers were gathering. "Like vultures," Pete muttered. Turning his attention to the growing traffic problem, he began to try to find a way to move cars around the scene. The truck driver had only scratches, and the State Patrol was busy taking his statement.

The injured man raised his head from the pavement and called loudly, "Does anyone here know how to pray?" Pete felt the queasiness return, but he quickly made his way back to the man on the road. As he approached, he heard the man say, "Then I'll pray 'meeself'." Pete's hardened eyes filled with tears as he heard this man so near death, begin to talk to his God. The tenderness, the closeness of the words were so unlike the cursing that frequented the fire station.

They evoked some new and strange emotion in Pete as he listened. Then Pete's sadness deepened as he watched the man's life slip away.

Having finished her book keeping work at the conference center, Mrs. Winifred Rupel made her way to the bus stop in the village of Cannon Beach. This was the kind of day that made her sorry to have to leave the comfortable breezes of the coast. But, she had committed herself to a meeting in Portland today, and so she settled her grandmotherly bulk onto a bench to wait for the bus. Her hair, now a regal white, was held tidily in a fashionable chignon. Her soft plump skin began to perspire in the heat. Surely, she thought, the same sun would make the city heat oppressive. Still, she hoisted herself up the bus steps and settled in for the now familiar ride up the Sunset highway.

It would be a long, slow trip. There would be many stops along the way. Winifred studied the magazine she brought along. Suddenly the bus ground to a stop. From the long line of cars ahead, Winnifred was sure there must be an accident. Checking her watch, she recalculated the time it would take to get to Portland. Accidents were terrible things to see. She hoped to pass the scene quickly.

Minutes passed. Progress was slow. The temperature in the bus climbed. Cars filed by the bus in long slow chains. The bus inched forward as they took turns using one lane around the accident. Everyone in the bus was becoming impatient. As they neared the scene, Winnifred glanced up from her magazine, and was surprised to see a car she thought she recognized. Surely it wasn't Archie's crimson Kaiser!

6

Then as the bus drew nearer still, her surprise turned to horror as she saw a body lying still on the highway. Partially covered, with people standing all around it, she was unable to be sure in passing. It appeared to be her beloved employer, Mr. McNeill.

"Wait," she called out, moving quickly up the aisle, "You must stop — please—" she implored. "I know that man —please— you must let me off here."

The driver would not stop. Anxious and tearful, Winifred got off the bus at the next village on the bus route. In desperation and fear, she made a phone call back to the coast.

It was unusual for Evangeline's brothers to be at the conference center together. It was even more unusual to have her sister from Missouri join them there. Evangeline Duff McNeill loved to have them all come. As children of immigrant parents, they had always been a very close family. Walter Duff, Jr., the oldest boy, was directing Village Missions from Dallas, Oregon. Haldane Duff, the baby of the family was a pastor in Seattle. Even Helen, the oldest of the Duff children, was involved in full-time Christian ministry. Their many speaking engagements, and the demands of their work kept them from coming to the coast to visit. But, this summer was different. By some delightful miracle, they all came to visit during the same week. Only their youngest sister Olive, who lived with her husband and family in California, was not with them.

So, when the conference receptionist brought a phone message to Walter, he was very surprised. Who would know to contact me here? he wondered. Excusing himself, he went to the phone booth in the lobby of the old log house to return the call. When he rejoined Edith, his wife, and his brother Haldane, he reported what little news he had. As yet, they were not even sure that it was Archie's little car on the highway. Together they agreed to hold Evangeline off while Walter made the necessary calls for more information. While Edith and Haldane stood blocking any view of the phone booth, Walter called hospitals, county and state police. No one had any information. Disappointed, he waited for a patrol officer's return call.

When the call finally came, the officer confirmed that Archie had indeed been in a terrible accident. He went on and on about the details of the accident. Impatient, Walter interrupted him, "But, what about Archie?"

"Oh," he returned flatly, "He's dead."

Evangeline was surprised that Archie had not returned by dinner-time. Mentally she went over his errand list, carefully calculating how much time each would require. Checking her watch again, she decided she would take his place at the evening prayer meeting, Whatever other prayer requests were made that evening, Evangeline had only one. "Bring Archie home safely Lord," she prayed. Was it her imagination or had that prayer bounced like echoes from the ceiling of the meeting room?

After prayer, Evangeline greeted the guests who had joined her. Then she walked outside to discover her entire family, in-laws and all gathered near the phone booth of the old log house. Before she could ask, Walter came toward her with anguish twisting the features of his face.

"Evangeline dear, I want to talk to you," he said, putting an arm around her. He walked her gently to the little cabin she shared with Archie. As she sat down on their bed, he told her as gently as he could of the accident.

"You mean he's gone?— he's dead?" She struggled to understand. He was so alive just this morning. Wanting not to believe, and yet seeing the truth in her brothers eyes, her own grief began. Tears began to flow down her cheeks. At last the realization came. She had lost her best friend, her lover, her sweetheart. He had been her pastor, her partner, and her favorite preacher. He was her favorite baritone. They had performed together, held meetings together, and prayed together. Together they had given birth to babies. They had laughed together. They had grieved together. She had meant to share life only with him. How could he leave her? Her sense of life purpose was wrapped up in him. Now, even now, all she could feel was emptiness—the deepest most painful and lonely emptiness she had ever felt. In him was everything she had ever wanted or needed. She was lost. How could she ever go on without him?

2

The Darkest Winter

For Evangeline, the winter of 1952 began on Tuesday, August 5th. For even in the August heat, she found herself in a cold, dark world without Archie. It was fortunate that her family was already at the conference center. Her shock and tears gave way to inconsolable weeping. After nearly two days, her desperate family sought the help of Evangeline's family physician. Medication helped her to rest for the days and decisions ahead. As Evangeline's mother took over the care of her two girls, and others cared for the guests of the conference center, Evangeline rested quietly in her room.

In quiet seclusion, she relived much of the triumph and grief of their past years together. Since the purchase of the conference center, they had been nearly constantly together. They had planned, dreamed, and worked on every aspect of the center. They had scrubbed and cleaned and painted. They had incorporated and renamed the historic building. They had prepared the outbuildings of the property to house additional guests. Together they had waited for the arrival of the first guests in July of 1945.

Surprised by the success of the work, they were

11

even more surprised when the following summer, guests came to Archie saying, "God's hand is on this work. We think you should build a dining hall." The men suggested using volunteer labor, inviting men to come to work for an organized "work week." It was the first of many such weeks. Each spring, men who believed in the ministry, gave of their time and skills to help the center grow.

For this first project, God brought an engineer and a builder to supervise the work. Fondly, Evangeline remembered cooking huge meals for the work crews. How she and Archie had looked forward to their arrival and enjoyed their enthusiastic support. She remembered Archie taking pictures of crews and helping where he could. He always wanted to be part of the action. Memories brought tears. And tears prevented sleep.

She remembered too the joy of Helen Jean's birth. They had wondered if they would ever have another child. But what a thrill to bring their new baby girl home to the center at the village by the sea. Helen was now only three years old—too young to understand what had happened to daddy. How would Evangeline tell her? How could Evangeline explain what she struggled so to understand herself.

Isabelle, their oldest, was 13. She adored her father. Archie had a special understanding for her—a special gift. Isabelle and Archie were connected in a way that mystified Evangeline.

How could Evangeline fill Archie's shoes. There would be no substitute. How could she support the girls herself? There was no money. There had been no salary. Every penny had gone back into expansion of the conference center.

For Evangeline, the depth of her grief had reduced her faith to simple and frequent cries for help. What would she do? How could she carry on without him? What would happen to the work? Over the next few days, hundreds of letters from all parts of the world came to the conference center. Telegrams arrived every few minutes. The grounds swelled with people from all over the northwest who came to Cannon Beach in response to Archie's death. There were members of their old Portland Church, people from the Service Men's Center where Archie had ministered during the war, business and civic leaders from everywhere.

Evangeline sensed their presence, their support, their prayers. Her sister Olive came from California to join the family. Somehow, Evangeline was able to help her brothers and sisters plan two services for Archie. One was held on the grounds at Cannon Beach. The other at the funeral home in Portland. She managed somehow to tape the services so that she could send tapes to Archie's mother in England. The activity was a tonic to her. Gradually she came more and more to be herself.

Having survived the funeral and burial services, the future looked bleak to Evangeline. The loneliness set in like an anvil on her chest. She longed to care about the work of the conference center. But everything about it reminded her that Archie was gone. She continued to pray for help. But each day was cold, and dark, and lonely.

Frequently, her thoughts returned to the conflict she was experiencing in her heart. After the funeral,

Doctor J. Vernon McGee took her aside. "It is a great work you do here, and it must continue," he said. "It is one of the most unique Bible conferences in the entire nation. However, it is clearly not the work of a woman." Dr. McGee had paused to let the words sink in. "Evangeline, Archie is gone and now you must get a man in here to do it."

How could she give away the work. It was Archie's— hers—theirs. To give the leadership away would be to give away the baby they had conceived. Evangeline had been trained for ministry from the time she was old enough to understand the gospel. To her father, there was no difference between men and women in the kingdom of God. If a person could speak, a person could minister the Gospel of Jesus Christ. Whether that person be man or woman made no difference to Evangeline's father. He felt that all Christians would be needed— male and female —to reach the world for Christ.

Now, it was hard for Evangeline to see things any other way. The more she considered it, the more she knew. Archie was gone. But Jesus was not. Jesus was the one who had given this dream to her. He was the one who had brought them this far. And in the end, only He would be able to take the dream the rest of the way. She was full of sadness and grief. But she would not quit. Taking pencil in hand, she wrote the rough draft of what would become the conference center's fall newsletter:

"I've thought about it so many, many times, in the daytime and at night and in the middle of the night. I know what God would have me do— continue! I know what dear Archie would have me do— continue! The

14

conference board met at the close of the season and agreed we should surely press on in this work which God has blessed so singularly in these past eight years. Do pray that God will give me the wisdom and strength to carry on this ministry."

Evangeline understood what she would do, but the problem of how she would do it remained. How could she support herself during the long winter ahead? The cold, rainy Oregon coast was not conducive to winter conferences. Her only source of winter income had been the meetings she and Archie had held for various churches along the west coast. Until Isabelle was of school age, she too had traveled with them. After she started school, Isabelle stayed with family friends in Glendale, Oregon. How could Evangeline support herself, the girls and the conference center alone?

Evangeline's family was asking the same question. They encouraged her to carry on the work of the center. They had watched its dream birthed and nurtured. They would do whatever was needed to see her bring it to maturity.

The week after Archie's funeral was a summer conference for the Christian Women's Council and Clubs. Helen was the supervisor of the conference. As she watched her sister Evangeline and the ladies who came to the center, suddenly, the answer came to Helen. She wasted no time presenting her idea to the family.

"Evangeline has always been instrumental in starting women's clubs and councils. No one knows how to help those ladies get started better than Evangeline.

Our ministry desperately needs her help. She could come back to Missouri and spend the winter at our headquarters with us. We would be able to pay a small stipend and send her out speaking to and organizing new groups all over the United States. We have more requests for help than we could ever fill on our own. It's the perfect place for Evangeline."

It seemed like an answer from heaven to Evangeline. It would give her some financial help, and leave her free to administrate the summer conference schedule. Best of all, it would give her a break from the loneliness of the dark, wet Oregon winter.

Helen, who now administrated the rapidly growing Christian Business and Professional Women's Council and its co-organization Youth Home Missions, had moved her headquarters to Kansas City in the spring of 1952. After six years in Fort Wayne, Indiana, the need for office and living space had forced them to look for a new and larger location. God had miraculously supplied a seven-and-one-half acre parcel complete with seventeen room house, stables and greenhouse.

In 1949, the Women's Council spawned a new ministry called Village Missions. Evangeline's brother, Walter Duff, Jr., resigned his church pastorate in Sunnyside, Washington to supervise the new work, which had as its goal supplying small rural communities with qualified pastors. Once again, the Duff family was training and sending workers into the vast rural field.

Evangeline's mother, Mathilda Duff, had been living with her children in various locations since the death of her husband in 1947. She was now in her seventies. Archie's death gave Mathilda a new determination, a new sense of purpose. Now she was needed off the screen porch housed the office space. The main floor provided the common living area. The staff had private rooms on the second floor. Evangeline, her mother, and her two daughters were given renovated servant's quarters on the third floor. The house was huge and beautifully decorated, with lush carpets and elegant rooms. Both Helen Jean and Isabelle quickly settled in. The office staff adopted them all as family. Mother Duff busied herself caring for the girls and helping wherever she was needed.

Certainly, life in Missouri was a diversion for Evangeline. She loved the travel involved with her new position. She was eager to get new councils started. She loved people; and she loved bringing others to the Lord. What a joy to be able to do the things she enjoyed most of all. Working with Christian Women's Clubs was very satisfying.

But in spite of demanding ministry, there were dark hours. Returning to Stonecroft from long and exhausting trips, Evangeline found herself alone again. There was no place where she could return to Archie. Though she was home with her girls; he was not. The reminded her of him. The mail reminded her of Every delivery was filled with letters of condo-

There was nowhere she could escape her grief. during the long lonely Kansas nights, Isabelle often her mother weeping.

mail, Evangeline did her best to care for the of the conference center. She wrote to the care-and to the conference treasurer every week. She brother Walter, who was still living in Oregon, whatever she could not.

again. Evangeline needed her. Her granddaughters needed her. She determined to make the trip across the United States with Helen and Evangeline's oldest daughter to Hickman Mills, Missouri. She would enter Isabelle in the school system and wait for Walter to bring Evangeline and little Helen Jean later in the fall.

That September brought a difficult experience for Evangeline. She watched with sadness as her mother and sister Helen left the conference grounds with Isabelle. Isabelle was Evangeline's connection to Archie. Somehow that parting, even though she knew she would soon be following behind, seemed to tear open the pain of her loss again.

Evangeline turned her energy to readying the grounds for the coming winter. She had a couple who would serve as caretakers. There was Jake the handyman. There was also John Goodmanson, who, from his home in Portland, took care of all the major finances. He accepted donations for the Conference Center. He kept records and provided year-end receipts. Certainly there was support for the ministry. But, still it seemed an insurmountable task to coordinate and supervise their work from Kansas City. She hated to leave.

As she was preparing to leave, the Cannon Beach School Board notified her that they would be demolishing the old school building located across the street from the conference grounds. They unanimously voted to award the building to the center for the price of $1—if it could be removed by the required deadline. This notification was quite a surprise to Evangeline, as she and Archie had bid for the building the previous winter. Hoping to use the building's lumber, they had offered the school board $1500.00. Their bid was refused because the amount was "too small for consideration." The school board notice was only one more pressure for Evangeline. Her maintenance man assured her that the building couldn't be removed within the allotted time. Reluctantly, she resigned herself to missing out on the valuable lumber.

Walking along the grounds shortly afterward with her brother, Haldane Duff, she showed him the school building they almost had for $1.

"Evangeline," he said, "it would be a sin to refuse such a wonderful gift."

Haldane was not dismayed by the enormity of the project. He was quite sure the building could be disassembled and the lumber moved. Men from Central Bible Church in Portland were scheduled to be at the conference grounds on Labor Day Weekend. Haldane boldly asked the men's group for volunteers. He recruited volunteers from his own church. He arranged crew supervisors for both a morning and afternoon shift. As dawn rose on Labor day, 1952, 22 men started to work. The crews continued until dark. Hammers, wrecking bars and saws worked continually. Men sorted, and stacked, and transported the lumber from wrecking sight to conference grounds. In one day, the building was brought down.

There was building material everywhere. The school district gave them 30 days to remove it. So, every weekend for four weeks, Haldane arrived in Cannon Beach with a new crew of men to remove the debris. By the end on the month, the entire pile had been transferred to the conference center grounds.

The lesson Evangeline learned was more than power of volunteer labor. She saw the hand of continuing to guide the work of the conference cer She also realized, in a new way, what it meant to be of the Duff family. Certainly, they were committ one another as brothers and sisters. Yes, they ha through difficulties and trials together. But, the more than that. They were a family of burden They did more than to talk support for one They lived out their support. As she watched brother pull boards away from the pile of lu realized again what a treasure God had giver way of family. She could trust them. She co them. Perhaps she was not as alone as she felt.

So it was with a mixture of emotions th left Cannon Beach, Oregon with Walter ar Jean. The changing of seasons brough changes for Evangeline. In a way, she fel was leaving Archie behind. He woul every building, in every ocean sunset a It was almost unbearable to leave hi work, if only for the winter. But, at th was anticipation. She was excited t and mother and her sister Helen forward to new work. New travel

Stonecroft. This was the name Women's Councils and Clubs hea Hills, Missouri. Miraculously, th been acquired in the spring of staff of seven were living in th

That dark winter, there were attempts to remove Evangeline as director of the conference center. Few believed that a woman could — or indeed should— be in charge of such an important ministry. Some tried to convince Walter to ask her to step down. He was the wrong person to convince. Walter believed in Evangeline. He was sure that God had chosen her to lead the conference center. No objection to Evangeline's leadership, however well intentioned, was kindly received by Walter Duff, Jr.

In the depth of the Missouri winter, Evangeline was making plans for an Oregon summer. She scheduled speakers, retreats, musicians. By the time the cold gave way to thaw, Evangeline Duff McNeill had begun to see the work as her own. If God had called her, as she believed He had, then He could be trusted to help her complete the job. Now, though her grief continued, she had a new sense of determination and purpose.

It was this new woman, this tried and stronger woman who left the mid-west in the spring of 1953. Evangeline headed to the Oregon coast with her two daughters and her mother, determined to see God fulfill a dream at Cannon Beach.

Isabelle, now 14, had been through a long, lonely winter as well. Though her grandmother tried, no one could soften the loss she felt. Her father had understood her. They rode horses together; spent time together. She had been ripped from the home she knew on the Oregon Coast and transplanted to the desolate, flat, drylands of Missouri. It was difficult to say the least. As she traveled back to the coast, Isabelle marveled at the woman who was her mother. Isabelle had been so focused on her father, that her mother was someone she didn't really know. It was time for that to change. Who was this woman? she wondered. Where did she come from? What gave Evangeline McNeill the kind of grit that enabled her to overcome such incredible adversity? Isabelle was determined to find out.

3

A Soul Is Born

Though Walter Duff was feeling quite ill this Sunday morning, he wondered how he would spend his time. In 1892, the State Church of Northern Ireland permitted few Sunday activities. The rest of his family was going to church. Oh well, he thought, I'll find something to do.

He turned away from his bedroom window just as the family buggy rounded the corner out of sight. The large Georgian-style home seemed strangely empty with the family away to church. Nearing 20 years old, Walter's life was filled with the family business. The three brothers had been groomed to manage the family linen mill, farms and wool holdings. They were a wealthy Irish family. Their entire village looked to them for economic stability. It wouldn't do for him to idle away his time. He looked around for something acceptable for Sunday reading. Spying a copy of the British Christian Herald, he settled in to the large chair by the fire. An article by the American preacher, Charles DeWitt Talmidge caught his attention. Soon he was absorbed in every word.

When the afternoon brought the Duff family home from church, they found a changed Walter. Charged with excitement, he explained what had happened to him. He described his morning's adventure with Dr. Talmidge. The article made it clear to him. He needed forgiveness of sins. He had asked for and now possessed eternal life.

James and Mary Duff were more than surprised by their son's revelation. "But Walter," his father protested, "Of course we're Christians. Don't we give the main support to the church?"

Disappointed, Walter realized that his family could not understand the great truth of his experience. Undaunted, he continued to share his story with others. Surely, he thought, our minister will understand. But the minister greeted his announcement with a strange, polite coldness.

The urge to tell others was more than Walter could resist. Soon large signs appeared on the walls of his father's mills. "Ye must be born again," they said. "PREPARE TO MEET THY GOD"

Though embarrassed by his son's new zeal, Walter's father tolerated it. He allowed Walter to hold spiritual meetings for the workers. They went on this way until one morning, three years later, when Walter entered his father's study. "Father," he said, "I must speak with you. It is of great importance."

James Duff listened carefully while Walter explained as best he could. "Father, I need to serve God full time- to be a pastor or an evangelist- I'm not sure. I only know that God has called me and I must go."

This was more than the elder James Duff could endure. "No Walter. You must stay with the firm. You

are the one with energy and drive. I cannot let you go."
His father was adamant. Several days later James called
his son to him. He loved his son, and earnestly desired
to resolve the conflict between them. "Walter," he said,
"if you will remain with the firm, I will contribute the
money to fully support two missionaries through your
entire lifetime. You cannot do more than two people,
can you?

"But, father," Walter answered firmly, deliberately, "God has called me and I must go."

Though his father threatened to leave him penniless, Walter persisted. And in the end, Walter's father
helped him attend Bible School in Glasgow, Scotland.

His commitment to full-time ministry had cost him
greatly. He was largely disinherited, penniless, and
separated from the love and approval of his family.
Still his only concern was for the souls of men who
knew nothing of the Saviour. Finishing school, he returned to Ireland and began to preach the gospel everywhere. Great crowds came to hear him, and many
responded to his message of Good News. Walter was
a young man, with a large nose and dark eyes, and a
tall slim build. It was clear that people flocked not just
to hear Walter Duff but to respond to the Holy Spirit
who was working through him.

Seeking a way to more effectively reach people, he
organized the Irish Christian Worker's Union. He chose
dedicated, talented, young men and women for instruction in the Bible, and in prayer. Thus prepared,
they were given many opportunities to preach throughout
Ireland.

Mathilda Hamilton was one of these young persons. Her parents had died while she was in her early

teens, leaving her to live with a maternal aunt. It was in her aunt's home that she came to know her Savior. In spite of her difficult life, she committed herself to full-time missions work. Mathilda applied to serve as a missionary to Africa, and was turned down. Her health was considered too delicate for the African climate.

Determined to serve, Mathilda applied and was accepted to the Christian Worker's Union. There she met Walter Duff. Her own deep love for the Savior was evident and attractive to Walter. She too was Irish. Her lovely deep brown eyes, dark hair and tiny figure were attractive to him as well. Together their zeal for evangelism multiplied. After some time, they became engaged.

On March 1, 1901, Mathilda Hamilton married Walter Duff. They took a brief honeymoon in Loch Lomond, Scotland and returned home to pour themselves into their work.

The turn of the century was a time of great revival in the British Isles. Unfortunately, mainline churches were not receptive to evangelists. Presbyterian churches were closed to the Union's young preachers, who were in the church's eyes largely untrained. So to reach people, Walter and Mathilda rented large country homes, enabling the young preachers to stay with them and bicycle to nearby meeting halls and school houses where services were held.

Great things were happening in Ireland, although the Irish revival of this period followed the Welsh revival with less intensity. Still large numbers of people responded to the gospel. Walter continued to plan conventions at holiday resorts such as Grants' Causeway and Portrush. Special trains were engaged to transport the enormous crowds who came only for the day. Often as many as five thousand people would attend.

The spiritual awakening was so great that it was said, "There is hardly a person in all Northern Ireland who cannot explain the simplicity of the grace of God." The revival itself provided financial support for the training and sending out of the Union's young missionaries.

While they organized and trained the young evangelists, Walter and Mathilda had four children. Helen, the oldest, Alexandra (who came to be known as Evangeline Duff McNeill) Walter, and Olive. Mathilda's health was fragile in those days and she was occasionally in bed. But her love for her children, combined with her deep love for Jesus, made her an extraordinary mother. In the evening the children would gather around her bed for story time. She would read them a Bible story or a missionary's adventure. As soon as she finished the children would chorus, "Tell it mother!" With theatrical animation she would embellish the story with great excitement and wonderful details. The children loved those evenings.

With many large and beautiful rooms, the great houses rented by the Duff family were situated on beautifully-landscaped grounds. Many times a groundskeeper was employed by the owner to care for the land. Mathilda often took the children for long walks along the country hedges. An artist herself (Mathilda had displayed many of her early paintings in London), her eye for color, beauty and texture was a source of much discussion and instruction for the children. Together they identified wildflowers and bulbs, and enjoyed the fresh air and exercise.

From her own family, Mathilda brought a great love and talent for music. Her father had been a church choir director and her sister a famous singer, known as "the sweet singer of Londonderry." Mathilda played the auto harp and the small family organ. She tried to share her passion for music with the children— and as youngsters they sang hymns together around the little organ.

The young preachers trained by Reverend Duff easily found pastoral positions all over the English speaking world. Many immigrated to the United States. They wrote frequently to Walter urging him to come to America. "There is multiplied opportunity here," they assured him. Repeatedly, he refused to go. Still the letters came. Gradually, he began to consider such a move. At nearly forty years old, Reverend Walter Duff finally decided to move to the United States. He would go alone to find a pastoral position. After settling in, he would make arrangements for his family to follow.

It wasn't easy for him to leave his young family. Never had he been separated from Mathilda. His oldest child was only nine. How he hated to go. Yet, he sensed the strong hand of God moving him toward the United States.

Walter Duff's ship took only three-and-one-half days to reach New York. Through an Irish pastor in Minneapolis, Walter found and accepted the pastorate of the International Falls Baptist Church. International Falls, Minnesota, was a small community of about 1000 Swedish immigrants fresh from the old country. The town was located very near the Canadian border, marked by the Rainy River. The river separated International Falls from its Canadian counterpart, Fort Francis, Ontario. This community too, needed a pastor. So, Walter Duff preached in the American church on Sunday mornings and after rowing himself across the river, preached at the Canadian church on Sunday evenings. In International Falls, he found an old wood frame house large enough for his family and began making plans to bring them to the United States.

At last the perfect opportunity presented itself. "Unsinkable" she was called. "The fastest ship afloat." Launched in 1911, built by Harland-Wolf in his own beloved Belfast, the Titanic was the hottest news of the year. Her enormous size, speed, and unsurpassed grandeur made Walter even more convinced. His family would enjoy the Titanic's inaugural cruise, scheduled for April 11, 1912. She would surely bring Walter's beloved family swiftly and safely to his side. With great anticipation, he made arrangements for their passage.

4
In God's Hands

At home in Ireland, Mathilda found herself desperately missing Walter. Though he had always provided a servant to help with the children, being alone made their care a more serious burden.

How delighted she was when she received Walter's wire with plans for her passage to America. She began to fill her lonely hours with the packing and sorting of their household goods. Eagerly she awaited the April sailing date.

However, in February 1912, the sudden news of a coal strike in England dampened her plans. The *Titanic*, scheduled to leave from Southhampton, England, would not sail until the strike was over. Father wired again. "Change plans," he said, "Sail from Londonderry."

Walter was determined not have his family's trip delayed. Not only would another ship sail immediately, but new plans would make the trip easier for Mathilda. She would not have to manage getting the four young children from Ireland to Southhampton, England alone. She made new plans, wired Walter, and purchased passage on the steamship *Scandinavia*, a ship of only 17,000 tons.

It was a disappointment to miss sailing on the

century's "greatest engineering feat." Her family was not rich, and trips abroad would not be a regular part of their lifestyle. Mathilda had heard of the *Titanic's* rich interiors, and private decks. All of Europe was kept abreast of the 66,000 ton vessel's completion. The ship would sail with the world's wealthiest families aboard. The passenger list included John Jacob Astor, the Vanderbilts and many others. The largest manmade object in the world, the *Titanic* was filled with handcarved wood, electric chandeliers, ballrooms and restaurants. It would have been a wonderful experience. Still, she was eager to join her husband as soon as possible. The coal strike would not delay the sailing of a smaller vessel. She determined to joyfully cross the Atlantic on whatever vessel was available.

At last, spring brought the day of departure. Though the *Scandinavia* was a small ship, it was freshly painted. The family found their tiny quarters comfortable. Once at sea, however, they were plagued by seasickness. Mathilda and her daughter Alexandra, nearly eight, spent most of the trip confined to their cabin. The other two children under big sister Helen's watchful eye, had free run of the small ship. And run they did. They spent their time in endless deck races and adventures. Before long, they were fast friends with both crew and passengers. Mathilda was grateful that Helen was a capable child. She was even more grateful to have the children away from the cabin.

Despite her hope that the passage would be swift, the ship traveled slowly. Three days, five days, seven days. The trip dragged on. The seasickness would not abate. Then, suddenly, in mid-Atlantic, the ship began stopping frequently. Checking in with mother, the children reported the strange actions and worried expressions of the crew. "Taking water temperature," they reported, "to watch for icebergs." What began as a leisurely passage slowed to a snail's pace.

Suddenly the engines stopped again.

This time, the children brought disappointing news. Because of the coal strike, the *Scandinavia* set sail from Ireland with less than a full supply of fuel. The frequent stops and slow passage used up the supply. Without fuel, they were forced to wait mid-ocean for more coal.

Somehow, the days passed and they were underway again. After 14 long days they reached the port of Halifax, Nova Scotia. This was their first scheduled stop, where passengers bound for Canada would disembark. It was not until they docked, that Mathilda learned of the *Titanic's* sinking. After the *Scandinavia* left Ireland, the *Titanic* sailed. Because of her speed, the *Titanic* had nearly caught up with the *Scandinavia* when she sank. The captain of the *Scandinavia* had heard of the sinking mid-voyage, on the new Marconi invention called the "wireless." It was the shocking catastrophe of the *Titanic* that prompted him to test carefully for icebergs. The *Scandinavia* sailed only three hundred miles from the location of the *Titanic's* sinking.

Mathilda was overwhelmed with the news. All of Halifax was draped in mourning as a reminder of the tragedy. By the time the *Scandinavian* docked, two vessels were appointed to leave Halifax to recover the bodies of *Titanic's* victims. Coffins were stacked in rows along the docks of the shipping line waiting to be loaded onto the search ships. Of the nearly 1700 passengers and crew that sailed on the Titanic, only 800 survived.

The depth of the story was only beginning to unfold when Mathilda reached Nova Scotia. Twenty lifeboats had been on board the *Titanic*. As she sank, most of the boats left the ship nearly empty. The third class fare for Mathilda's family would have been $20. Only a handful of the Irish immigrants sailing third class survived the sinking. Mathilda was deeply grateful for the protecting hand of her God. Though she was exhausted from her own seasickness, she could not help but pray and wonder as she looked at each of her own children, for what divine purpose had they been so miraculously spared?

5

The New Land

Boston, Massachusetts, was the last stop for the *Scandinavia*. For weary Mathilda and her four small children it was a wonderful relief to disembark their floating home. Boston's harbor was filled with ships and her streets were crowded with new arrivals.

Mathilda shuffled the children through customs, where an irritable customs officer made fun of their traditionally long family names. " Who do you think you are?" he smirked, "Royalty?"

She turned her tearful eyes away from him. Seeing her fatigue, and the burden of her solitary crossing, he stamped her papers quickly.

"Lady, you have an honest face."

Alone, Mathilda discovered all the hotel rooms in Boston were taken. She found space in the lobby of a city hotel, where she and the children were able to spend the night. The next morning they boarded the train that would take them to meet father.

There was more joy in that single reunion than the train station at International Falls had ever witnessed. Embracing each child in turn, and finally Mathilda, Walter's eyes spilled over with relief and gratitude.

Not one corner of the globe had missed the details of the *Titanic's* sinking. After the first news of the disaster, father had read every word of every newspaper he could find. He followed the first accounts of "slight damage—all passengers saved." When finally the true dimension of the tragedy was revealed, he too had been overwhelmed with the goodness of God's protection for his family.

At last they were together. Determined that his young family would never be separated again, Walter guided the horse and buggy to their home in this new land.

International Falls, Minnesota, a town of about 1000 people was located 275 miles due North of Minneapolis. It was a land of lakes, rivers and deep forests. It was a wilderness that terrified Mathilda, having grown up in the dense urban area of Ireland. It was some comfort to her that their home was located in town.

The people too were a bewilderment. The Irish were private and close-mouthed. It was very difficult for her to adjust to the outspoken and sometimes crude manners of the Swedish immigrants. With time, she found them kind and thoughtful. She grew to love them deeply.

The following year passed quickly for the Duff family. The two congregations on either side of the border grew to love their new pastor and his talented wife. There were church picnics and long walks amidst the deep forests. The children played in many vacant lots. Tall lithe Indians were part of their daily experience.

Close friendships developed. An Episcopal minister befriended the family with frequent visits and gifts. A lonesome bachelor, he enjoyed the company of a lively family. He often brought fresh maple syrup. On one visit, he taught the children how to roll clumps of syrup in the snow, and shape and pull the syrup into candy.

With the first winter came the delightful anticipation of another Duff baby, to arrive in the spring. The children were excited — at last a child born in the United States — a real American.

On May 21, 1913, Haldane Duff was born. The small rural hospital was located only a few blocks from their International Falls home. So, Helen would daily lead her brood of brothers and sisters to visit mother and the new baby. How glad they were when at last mother and baby were able to come home.

By now the children were old enough to read. Mother organized an "evening reader" while the children did the dishes. Taking turns, they all grew to love the works of Charles Dickens, Robert Louis Stevenson and many others. As each month progressed, the family began to feel more truly a part of their new surroundings.

However, in the fall of 1913, Walter became greatly concerned about Mathilda. The Midwestern winter was severe and had already taken its toll on her. Mathilda was frequently confined to bed, and her fragile health worsened. Helen and Alexandra, being only ten and nine, took as many household responsibilities as they could. But still, all began to fear for the life of their mother. Father began to ask everyone he knew, "Where in the United States is there a mild climate like Ireland?" His research pointed him toward the Pacific Northwest. Friends of members in his Fort Francis church put him in contact with an Irish pastor of the First Baptist Church in Oregon City, Oregon. Dr. Millikan arranged for Portland's Calvary Baptist Church to hear Reverend Walter Duff. In 1914, he was called as their pastor.

In the spring of that year, the Duff family again packed their belongings and traveled by train to Hood River, Oregon. Here Reverend Duff filled a temporary summer pastorate waiting for the Portland position to open. By fall, the Duffs were settling into Portland and their second American pastorate.

The mild Oregon climate was everything Reverend Duff hoped it would be. But he found himself deeply disappointed in the Christians living on the west coast. Walter's heart beat for the unsaved, and try as he would, he could not persuade his congregation to take up the job of winning souls. All of Portland seemed to him to be in a "spiritual slump."

Everywhere Reverend Duff went, he was confronted with the need for people to hear about Jesus. Though others refused to share their faith, Walter was determined to do everything he could to spread the Good News. So one afternoon in 1918, Reverend Duff took his son Walter, Jr. with him on a streetcar into downtown Portland.

"Walter," the elder Duff said as he disembarked on Alder street, "There are men here on the street who need to know about Jesus." He bent to meet young Walter's eyes with his own. "And we are going to find a way to tell them. We are going to rent some space in a building, and hold services and have literature. It will be just what these men need. Today we are going to find the space God has for us to use."

So together, father and son tramped the sidewalks until at last they found office space at 3rd and Alder. Walter rented the building and began making plans for his new project.

Within months, he was pastoring one of Portland's largest and most prestigious churches, while at the same time managing a flourishing ministry to street people. Downtown, at "Hope Hall," he sold religious literature, and held both Sunday afternoon and evening services. Eventually, he taught several Bible classes there and began publishing a small weekly paper.

The Duff children loved to go to Hope Hall. Each week they eagerly accompanied their parents on the trip to town. Reverend Duff was a delightful and energetic preacher. No one admired him more than his five children who faithfully took their places on the front row at Hope Hall.

To the Oregonians in Reverend Duff's congregation, their new Irish pastor seemed a different sort—he had such a serious regard for his faith. They were taken back by his straight-forward zeal. Still, his delightful sense of humor and deep love for people won him to their heart.

In the midst of this first year in Portland, Mathilda became ill again. Confined to bed, she continued to love and lead her family. In spite of bedrest, the disease grew worse. At last she and Walter returned to the doctor.

All of Portland seemed damp and grey when finally the two returned home. The children recognized the fear in their mother's eyes as she came in the parlor door. With tender care, father prepared her tea and carried her upstairs to bed. Somehow, the children knew. Silence filled the house as they waited for father to come downstairs again.

"Children," he said gathering them together around the large kitchen table, "the doctor says your mother has consumption. He says she will not live much longer. Mother is afraid because your grandmother died of consumption." He paused to let the children understand his words. Then through his own tears, he looked at each face in turn. "But," he continued, "the doctor does not know about Jesus. So, we will pray. We will ask Jesus to spare your mother's life. We will ask and believe," he said, " and then we will trust Him."

So as the rain fell outside, small tears fell inside. Together five small children and one desperate husband prayed earnestly for the life of the woman so precious to them.

Darkness fell. The rain stopped. But the prayers continued. At last, Walter lit the hall lamps and lead the sleepy tribe to bed. Lovingly, he said goodnight to each. "Jesus hears our prayers" he promised. "We will see."

Weeks passed. Gradually it seemed that the worst was over. Mathilda's strength returned slowly. A grand celebration accompanied her first dinner in the big kitchen.

With the joy of Mathilda's returning health, Walter could again concentrate on the work of the church and of Hope Hall. Things were happening downtown. People responded to his messages. Walter found many who were eager to know more about the good news he proclaimed. Once again, his love of evangelistic work came to life. He felt the desire to leave the pastorate and concentrate again on evangelistic work.

But now, with his large family, how could he move into full-time evangelism? How could he leave the security of salary and parsonage? With much prayer, Reverend Walter Duff, Sr. resigned from Calvary Baptist. If God was the source of this new direction, how could he do anything else?

6

Operation Evangelism

Reverend Walter Duff heard the call to full-time evangelistic work. Still, he had a wife and five children to support. Determined to provide for his family as he followed the Lord's leading, Walter located a tiny church on Portland's east side. Tabernacle Baptist had been closed for years in need of a pastor. The Oregon State Baptist Committee agreed to let the Duffs live in the church's small parsonage if Walter would fill the pulpit and reopen the small church. They would even contribute $20 per month in salary.

For almost two years he occupied the pulpit of Tabernacle Baptist and continued his work at Hope Hall. He also began holding evangelistic meetings in nearby communities. At first, he traveled along the West Coast of Washington, Oregon and British Columbia. Later, as his territory enlarged, he began including his children in his work.

Never one with great concern for formal education, Walter would take the children out of school to travel with him. Helen, the oldest, now in her late teens, was the first to come along. Gradually his son Walter, and Alexandra were joining them as well. Mother, wanting the children to finish school, would find some need for one to stay at home with her. In this way, each completed high school, though the long absences made Alexandra nearly twenty before she graduated.

Father Duff had great passion for evangelistic work. Each of his children was trained in every area of public ministry. To him, it was clear that each child must be fully equipped to take on the work that so consumed him. They all could preach, lead the song service, and play any number of hymns. Mother supported the team by choosing special music. She trained the teenagers in instrumental and vocal duets and trios. As they were able, each of the children entered full-time evangelistic work.

One afternoon, shortly after returning from a trip with father, Alexandra entered his study. "What is it Alec?" father asked.

"Father, I need to speak to you of something important." She steadied herself. "I want to be called Evangeline. When we travel together, all of you use your pet names for me in public. I am too old to be called 'Alec,' father. My middle name is Evangeline, and I want to use it."

"Certainly, Evangeline." Father's eyes smiled at her. His daughter was becoming a lovely young woman.

Under father's watchful eye, the children's talents were carefully developed. Together they blended into a perfectly orchestrated, wonderfully effective team. After some time, Walter, Jr. began to hold services on his own. The three younger sisters joined forces to become the Duff Sisters Gospel Trio. Helen often preached and Evangeline lead the song services. In each location, they provided an afternoon children's program.

Here the children were trained to participate in the evening service. Whether a dramatic presentation, or music, families flocked to see the evening "performance" of their children.

Early on, the Duff Trio visited primarily rural communities without church programs of their own. Often these communities had old abandoned church buildings. The girls would obtain permission to use the buildings and spend whatever time and energy was necessary to clean and ready the auditorium for services.

Though it took many hours, the three sisters chose also to personally invite families in nearby homes to their services. Evangeline managed the trio's publicity. She designed fliers, wrote newspaper releases, and was constantly on the lookout for clever ways to draw townspeople to their services. Her sisters Olive and Helen never quite knew what to expect from Evangeline. But they were most surprised when they first spotted her latest technique. She had fit their little truck with long poles supporting a great banner announcing the trio. "What is that for?" Helen asked.

"We'll just have ourselves a little musical parade," she reported, her eyes merry with the fun of it. "Only we will be the whole parade!"

"Evangeline!" Olive gasped, "When? Where?"

"I think noon would be good," she replied, "right down mainstreet." The three young girls worked their way down mainstreet playing their instruments. They were talented, energetic and attractive in their tailored blue serge dresses with embroidered white collars and cuffs. The plan worked beautifully. Many townspeople attended that evening.

Their services were full of charm and humor. As a result they had no difficulty filling the small churches night after night. Many came to know the savior they so exuberantly served. Among denominations, word passed quickly that this young group was effective in bringing communities to Christ. Invitations to other towns and churches exceeded their ability to respond. Bigger churches in larger cities began to request their services. Soon they were holding city wide meetings in the largest of churches up and down the west coast.

It was their custom to greet their guests after each service. One evening in Eureka, California as she was shaking hands, Helen was surprised to find a small piece of paper folded and pressed into her hand. Without any clue as to its importance, she slipped the paper into her pocket. Later, she thought, I'll see what this is.

As they were traveling to their room that night, Helen passed the small paper to Olive. "Girl's look," Olive said excitedly, "It's a check. And I think it is made out for $500."

In the early 1920s, such a sum was so unheard of, so enormous, that Helen immediately pulled their little car off to the side of the road. In the dark, the three girls got out of their car to hold the check up to the car headlights. There was no mistaking the number. It clearly said five hundred dollars.

Together, they considered the situation. Surely someone had meant to write only five dollars. What would they do? The solution was simple. The next day they would all go to return the check to the giver. With the matter settled, they readied themselves for a well-deserved night's rest.

The next day the three girls began their investigation. With some persistence, they arrived at a tiny shack located near a county road building project. It was a hot day, and dust was everywhere. The gritty substance hung in the air and coated every item in the little hut.

In spite of their surroundings, R.G. and Evelyn LaTourneau greeted the girls with a bubbling enthusiasm that was refreshing all the way to the soul. "No, the check was no mistake," R.G. assured them. "It was just an expression of thanks for the great job you three are doing." And so, inspite of the heat and the dust, what followed was the beginning of a long and wonderful friendship between the two families.

After a time, they rented a house together. It was a respite for the LaTourneau family from the dust of the road project. For the girls, it provided a base of operation for their traveling ministry. Their friendship continued to blossom. From there, the LaTourneaus and the Duff sisters agreed to take a break from their work to study at the Bible Institute of Los Angeles (BIOLA). So, in 1926 with the financial support of the LaTourneaus, the group traveled south for the fall term.

It wasn't long before Helen desperately missed evangelistic work. She felt studying was taking time from the more productive work of winning souls. She continued to receive invitations to conduct services. Reluctantly, she left her two sisters behind to resume evangelistic ministry.

Olive and Evangeline, however, loved school. They studied hard and were successful in their classes. They attended the Church of the Open Door in Los Angeles, pastored by the renowned Scottish preacher John McNeill. Known as the Scottish "Spurgeon," McNeill had pastored the three largest congregations in the United States. His son, Archie McNeill, was also attending BIOLA. Many a weekend found a large group of students at the McNeill home for an evening of fun.

It wasn't long before Archie, a tall, roundish young man with a thick Scottish Brogue decided that Evangeline Duff was worth more of his attention. In the European way, he approached her about the prospect. But he was new in the United States (having only recently immigrated from Scotland), and Evangeline rejected his approaches.

"He's nice enough, and lots of fun," she later told her sister Olive, "It's just that he's so un-American. He's definitely not for me!"

By the end of their first term, R.G. LaTourneau decided that he was not a student at heart. Taking a job on a Florida road project, he urged Olive and Evangeline to follow along. The girls had no desire to travel to Florida, and no funds to continue school. So, with a shrug of the shoulders, they left BIOLA to return to the work they knew so well. They rejoined their sister Helen and her full schedule of meetings, happy to be together again.

A short time later, the girls were joined by a classically trained pianist named Charles Huddleston. His family background was similar to the Duffs, and he fit in well from the moment he joined them. His strong and powerful approach to the keyboard fit in especially well with Evangeline's charm and vocal abilities. Pastors recommended the team saying, "There isn't a soul in the house who can resist joining the fun of the singing." They traveled together for some time. The crowds continued to come. The cities and churches continued to request their services.

After a church service in San Jose, California, the girls were invited to the pastor's home. Many from the congregation were there, including a particular banker who seemed especially glad to meet Helen. Though the girls left town soon after the meeting, the resourceful banker, Elwood Baugh, would come to other meetings in distant towns, just to visit with Helen. In spite of a difficult courtship, he pursued and won her love. On January 23, 1928 they were married. Unfortunately, the schedule for the Duff Trio was so busy that it was nearly six months before Helen could return to San Jose to live with Elwood.

Before long, Charles Huddleston, the new pianist, decided that he was especially fond of another Duff sister. He and Olive were married on January 26, 1930.

With her two sisters happily married, the Duff sisters trio was no more. Walter Duff then asked his sister Evangeline to join him in his evangelistic work. Evangeline was glad to help. Haldane, her youngest brother, was now a young man. Occasionally he joined Walter and Evangeline. Once again there was an Irish trio! The three siblings traveled a broad area of the country together. Their talent, hard work, and commitment to prayer made them a successful team.

These were depression days. Poverty was rampant in the United States. People had no money and nothing to do. There were few distractions in the hard working lives of people in the rural communities. Evangelistic meetings were exciting happenings in small and large communities alike. The crowds continued to come.

Though others found these to be economically difficult days, Walter, Evangeline, and Haldane were never in need. Other evangelists of the day earned reputations as fraudulent scoundrels. For this reason, the Duffs were very careful to outline their financial policy before they agreed to come to a community. They would come for the amount of the nightly offering only. No promotion. No "Love Offering." They would take just one simple, quiet offering at each meeting. This the people found agreeable. And never, in all the turbulent economic times of the Great Depression, did the Duff Evangelistic Trio find themselves wanting.

One engagement found Walter and Evangeline in Roseburg, Oregon. Haldane left them to return to college. Rumor had it that a large concert harp, located on the second floor of an old theatre building, had been retained in lieu of rent from a previous theatre company. Evangeline normally accompanied herself using a small Irish harp. What an exciting possibility, she thought, to own a concert harp. It would make a wonderful addition to their music program.

Many tried unsuccessfully to buy the beautiful, full-sized Wurlitzer harp. Walter and Evangeline made arrangements with the owner to view the instrument. Even though it was now more than 20 years old, they were taken with its beautiful new condition. Together they asked him to consider selling it on a contract. No success. Subsequent visits, covered with prayer, seemed to change his mind—especially when he understood their intended purpose. Finally he agreed to sell.

Two hundred dollars was an enormous investment in those times. Faithfully, a monthly $10 or $20 payment was made, until at last the harp was their's. With much gratitude, Walter and Evangeline loaded the enormous harp onto the trailer which would be its traveling home. They were the Duff Trio again!

Together Walter and Evangeline traveled to city after city. As a direct result of their ministry, large numbers of people decided to trust in the forgiveness of Christ. Everywhere the Duffs encouraged believers to live fully for Christ. Together constantly, Walter and Evangeline grew to become the closest of friends. He came to respect her tremendous musical talent, her ability to communicate the gospel, and her head for administration. She admired his ability to preach, as well as his unaffected leadership and practical problem solving. Few brothers and sisters had such a unique opportunity to work together. They knew how special it was.

Then in 1933, Walter and Evangeline held services in Dallas, Oregon. There, in the Methodist church, Walter was introduced to a charming and lovely young school teacher. She had been raised in the church, though never quite sure of her own salvation. In these services, she came to truly understand what Christ had done for her. It was a life-changing realization.

Walter left Dallas. But, he didn't forget the lovely teacher. Eighteen months later, Edith Dunn received her first letter from the handsome evangelist. He was concerned about the difference in their ages, and he wanted to give her time to grow and develop her own talents. A long courtship followed.

The Duff family received many invitations to conduct meetings. The demand was so great, that Walter and Evangeline occasionally separated to meet the many requests. By 1936, Evangeline was traveling with Naomi Van Cleave, a friend of Walter's who studied dramatic presentation in college. She provided recitations and dramatic readings to the services. Evangeline lead the music and preached the messages. They were happy traveling together, and decided to purchase a mobile home and continue the work. Finding a truck with a home made shelter, the two set off to win the world to Christ.

The timing proved perfect. In June of 1936, Evangeline's older brother Walter Duff, Jr., married Edith Dunn. Edith and Walter chose to work together. Gradually, Walter settled into pastoral work.

Though Evangeline greatly missed Walter, she was pleased to have him marry Edith Dunn. The newlyweds were very happy together. What could explain the tinge of sadness she felt? Some important part of her was left behind with Walter. Something inside her longed for the happiness he found.

Evangeline continued to work with Naomi. She found contentment in the work she loved. Still, she wondered, is there someone special ahead for me?

7

Love at Last

In November of 1937, Naomi and Evangeline, now 33, decided to work their way toward California. The goal was San Jose, where Evangeline's sister Helen and her husband Elwood Baugh were planning to host a family Thanksgiving. Walter, Sr., and Mathilda were enjoying a California winter while staying in Helen's guest house. Haldane, now attending BIOLA, had invited school friends to join the holiday festivities. Evangeline's brother Walter brought Edith down from Oregon. It promised to be a wonderful family gathering.

Their first evening together was a delightful reunion. There was much catching up to do. Haldane's friends included his girlfriend, who was a skilled pianist, and their old friend Archie McNeill. After dinner music filled the big house, and hymn followed hymn amid laughter and gaiety. Late in the evening, Archie, an accomplished vocalist, reluctantly agreed to sing for them. His choice, "Son of my Soul," filled the living room in his rich baritone voice. Evangeline was moved by his beautiful rendition of the old hymn. But it was more than the performance that caught her attention. Somewhere deep in the heart of the singer something was changed. When last with Archie, Evangeline was quite sure he had made no real commitment to Christ. But now, every phrase carried the deep devotion of the singer. There was no mistaking the transformation. This was a Christ-filled life. But more than music was moving in Evangeline's heart. Even as she listened she found a deep love springing up inside for him.

Over the long weekend the six young people spent much time together. Each day found them out sightseeing. Once to the mountains, another trip to the conservatory, and always with a large picnic lunch. Each evening they returned hungry and happy to a meal prepared by Helen and Mathilda. For their contribution, Archie and Evangeline volunteered to wash dishes. Alone in the kitchen, the two enjoyed much conversation. In the eight years since they attended BIOLA together, Archie's father had resigned his Los Angeles church pastorate and returned to preach in the British Isles. Because Evangeline had not heard anything more from him, she assumed that Archie went to Europe with his family. But the story he told over dishes that weekend was quite different.

Leaving BIOLA, Archie began to earnestly study music and voice. His goal was opera. It was a long, difficult pursuit, fraught with the frustration of financial troubles. He worked hard to gain recognition in the entertainment industry. Joining a group of young men of different nationalities, each a soloist in his own right, they called themselves "The International Four." After much work, and generous critics, they gained success in Hollywood. Engagements, money, bright lights and notoriety were his. Archie was on his way.

While he pursued fame, Archie was the bass soloist for a Long Beach church choir. Special services,
conducted by Dr. John G. Mitchell, required his nightly
attendance. At the end of a service, late in the week,
Archie realized, "I am living a lie— son of the famous
Dr. John McNeill — a church member, a soloist— but
not a Christian." Dr. Mitchell gave an altar call that
night, just as he had each night before. Archie hesitated
a long time before responding. He heard the call to
salvation. But he also recognized the Holy Spirit calling him to a life of full-time service. It seemed like
hours passed as he wrestled with his decision. In the
end, only moments later, Archie came forward. His
heart responded with a resounding "yes."

The decision, though difficult to make, had an
overwhelming effect in his heart. Suddenly in love
with the Lord, Archie told everyone about his new
found happiness.

It was more difficult though, to tell the other members of the quartet. At last they were entertaining the
biggest names in Hollywood. How could he throw
away such opportunity for some service as yet un-
known? He was sure they wouldn't understand.

On one particular night, after entertaining the stars,
the quartet was invited to an exclusive Hollywood
nightclub. As the night progressed, so did the drinking
and carousing. The sight became embarrassing and
uncomfortable to the son of a minister. Archie knew he
didn't belong. The brazen drunkenness of the evening
gave him the courage he needed to make the break.

He was right. After working so hard to succeed, no
one in the quartet could understand Archie's willingness to throw it all away.

Archie was a bit disappointed as well. Now, with nothing left of his old life, how could he further follow the Lord? What was next? He was not sure. But he did know that the Lord would show him in due time.

Soon after, an old teacher friend of Archie's parents learned of his conversion. With some effort she found him in Los Angeles. He would need training to ready himself for ministry, she thought. Would he consider returning to BIOLA under her financial sponsorship?

Archie, hungry for God's divine direction, eagerly accepted the teacher's kind offer. This was the new Archie McNeill that Evangeline's brother, Haldane, found and invited home for the holidays.

The weekend was over all too soon. Evangeline waved Archie and Haldane away as they returned to BIOLA. How she wished they could continue her new friendship. Naomi and Evangeline stayed on in San Jose until Christmas. Daily she watched the mail hoping for some contact with Archie. At last a letter came— but only a thank you note to her parents.

Evangeline began to pray. This new interest in Archie was more than she wanted to handle on her own. As with everything, she submitted her hopes and desires, concerns and fears to her Lord in prayer. "Bring him back," she prayed fervently, "But only as a sign of your approval. Lord, if this is not for me— may I never see him again!" It took courage to pray that way. She loved Archie, and to see him again without having God's approval would be too painful. Again she waited.

At last Evangeline received a letter from Haldane. Having noticed her interest in Archie, Haldane wrote

As Archie slept, Evangeline contemplated the upcoming family gift exchange. Finding her mother in the guest house, she asked for advice concerning the appropriateness of a gift for Archie. With Mathilda's encouragement, Evangeline slipped away to select a shaving kit. She carried it home, and lovingly wrapped and placed it under the tree. Suddenly Christmas was exciting again.

Archie rose refreshed and happy, eager to join the festivities. But the sight of so many gifts under the tree concerned him. Pulling Evangeline aside, he said sheepishly, "I am not able to participate in gift giving. Perhaps I should not join you."

She reassured him that the family certainly understood the financial situation of students during depression days. A gift was not expected from him. After all, this was an exchange of gifts between family members. "But Archie, we want you with us to enjoy the fun."

Helen and Elwood had remembered all the guests with gifts. Archie had brought a box of chocolates for the family. There was much love, laughter and happiness that evening. When Archie was given his gift from Evangeline, he was surprised. But his pleasure was evident to anyone with eyes to see. He thanked Evangeline warmly and gently chided her about their earlier conversation.

The evening continued as before, but something was different. Archie's eyes followed Evangeline's every movement. After the late evening tea and dessert dishes had been cleared, and the last of the wrapping paper had been burned, it was time to say good night. Archie asked if he might walk Evangeline out to the guest house.

to let her know that Archie was writing regularly to a girl in Canada. "Don't think another thing about him," he advised, "He isn't available."

Disappointed, Evangeline prayed more earnestly. God knew how she felt. Certainly, He could handle all the details.

The end of the Thanksgiving holiday had been difficult for Archie as well. Evangeline was a remarkable woman. Mature, energetic, attractive and with such integrity in her relationship with her Savior. Archie found that she too had changed since her days at BIOLA. And in every way, he found the changes more attractive.

Evangeline was not the first woman Archie felt this about. In the years since he first attended BIOLA, he had broken an engagement. The experience was a troubling one. Now, Archie was an entirely different young man. His primary concern was following God's lead in his life. God had so dramatically brought him to BIOLA; Archie reasoned that the same God could clearly confirm His direction in choosing a wife.

So Archie resolved not to contact Evangeline. He began to pray. It was his earnest desire to return to San Jose and Evangeline for Christmas. But Archie had no money and no means of transportation. This was the great depression. More than 500 miles separated them. It seemed an impossible wish.

"Lord, will you provide a way?" He prayed, "Or, I will know that she is not your choice for me." Because of a school choir tour, Archie was unable to work during the holidays. Without finances of his own, Archie watched his mail carefully. Always his family remembered him with a check at Christmas time. But, this season, his mail box was empty.

With the choir tour over, all of Archie's closest friends left school for home. Archie's hopes for a trip to San Jose seemed to slip away. In the echoing silence of the campus, he returned alone to his room. The last few cheery goodbys of his classmates only deepened his despair. He would not make any step toward San Jose unless God provided the way. This was how he had prayed. He would stick with his prayer.

In San Jose, preparations for Christmas kept Evangeline's hands occupied. But her thoughts never drifted far from Archie. Christmas vacation arrived and Haldane came to Helen's home alone. Though disappointed, Evangeline greeted him warmly. When they were alone together, Haldane told Evangeline, "I know you care for him Evangeline. But you must change your heart. He is in love with someone else."

Evangeline fought with her emotions. God knows, she thought, I can trust Him.

Archie too was fighting the sinking disappointment he felt. A knock on the door interrupted his thoughts. "Archie," his friend said cheerfully, "I heard you might be interested in a trip north. I'm headed for San Francisco. But, I'm so tired, there's no way I can drive up there myself. If you'll drive— you can come along for free." Archie eagerly agreed. Only hours later, he was driving north toward San Jose. To Evangeline.

Driving all through the night, Archie was alone with his thoughts. Suddenly he realized. What about Evangeline? There had been no affection. No indication. Could she care for him? She had not even written to him. What if his love were unreturned? How foolish he would feel.

Evangeline spent her days helping mother and Helen. But the season's decorating and baking lacked their usual fun and anticipation. Despite Haldane's warning, Evangeline found her thoughts constantly returning to Archie. Did he care? Would he return? Each thought prompted her to prayer. For Evangeline, a life partner would have to be God's choice. Over and over again, she carefully placed her hopes for the future in the hands of her loving God. He had met her every need these 33 years. Certainly she could trust Him now.

Then, one morning just two days before Christmas, Evangeline went to answer a knock at Helen's front door. There stood Archie, a giant of a young man, his hair disheveled, and his eyes red from sleepiness. His face though, was consumed by a merry smile. Suppressing her excitement, Evangeline escorted him inside.

"Something to eat, and a good rest is what you need," Evangeline assured him. And off she went to prepare a room. At last, striving to appear calm, she closed the door to Archie's room. He would sleep for quite some time. Her heart was full of thanks for God's guiding hand. She was quite convinced that His approval rested on her choice.

Along the path in the garden, he caught her elbow and turned her toward him. "Could we talk just a while?" he asked. Even in the moonlight she could see the concern and earnestness in his face. With careful detail, he relayed to her his prayer of the last five weeks. "I wanted to return, to contact you. But I was so afraid that you might not share the feelings I have for you." The words came in a rush. Taking a deep breath he began again, "But tonight, I think I know. Tell me, do you care?" His expression was tight in anticipation.

What a tender scene they made together in the clear December night. What joy to know that God had so divinely brought them together in this way. Yes, Evangeline cared. From that night forward she wrapped her entire being in the gentle and complete love that Archie held for her. As a woman, she had waited a very long time to hear these words. And now, she was ready. She was mature, confident, happy. Archie's love was, to her, a marvelous bonus of her already full life in Christ.

Yes, she cared.

8

Two Become One

Before breakfast the next morning, in typical English fashion, Archie approached Reverend Walter Duff, Sr., and requested the hand of his daughter Evangeline in marriage. The prospect of such a fine son-in-law delighted the older Irishman, and the twinkle in his eyes let Evangeline know what had transpired, even before Archie explained.

So sure were they of their love, that Archie and Evangeline made immediate plans for their wedding. Less than three weeks later, on January 28, 1936, they were married. Though they planned a church wedding, the sudden serious illness of their pastor forced them to change plans. They would not consider having another minister. Dr. Crouser had known the McNeill family since 1915. He was part of the committee that invited Dr. John McNeill to the Church of the Open Door in Los Angeles. Though he was too ill to leave his home, he conducted the McNeill wedding in his living room, assisted by Evangeline's father. It was a small private ceremony.

In 1936, the great depression was at its height. There were no pictures and few gifts to mark the wedding ceremony for Archie and Evangeline. But the national economy had little effect on their gayety of heart. Evangeline wore her best oyster white suit. Carefully tailored and fitting her slim figure beautifully, there was never a more radiant bride. Her mother, Mathilda, and sister Helen spared no effort in decorating Helen's home and garden with the flowers they so dearly loved. With the ceremony completed, they celebrated with friends, food and music at Helen's home.

Archie was beside himself with happiness. The beautiful redhead he had so admired ten years ago, was at last his own. His happiness was made even more complete by the deep and committed love she expressed for him. He would always treasure the message she wrote to him on the morning of the wedding:

"My own dear Archie,

This will probably be the last "love note" you receive from me before we are married. How happy I am dear, and how I love you. I admire your outstanding Christian qualities and on the other side your tender, loving spirit, and understanding ways. You have already made me so happy and I know the days to come will be "Pleasant paths." I know we shall face difficulties and troubles but together it shall be easier.

"The lovely fellowship and prayer we had together last night was something I shall never forget. Oh you are so dear to me... How proud I shall be to be called by your name this afternoon."

There was little time for a honeymoon after their wedding. Archie withdrew from BIOLA and the bride and groom became a new evangelistic team. At first, they traveled with Evangeline's brother Walter. Together, Walter and Evangeline helped Archie developed his preaching skills. He and Walter took turns giving the evening message. Always there to encourage and polish, Evangeline shared her own experience with her new husband.

Eventually, Evangeline and Archie were on their own. Music was their drawing card. His rich baritone voice was complemented by Evangeline's skill on the classical harp, piano and vibraharp. She provided variety by accompanying herself in singing the great hymns of the faith. They billed their work as "musicals," and Archie concluded every service with an evangelistic message.

In January, 1937, Evangeline's father began publishing the "Monthly Evangel", a magazine designed to publicize and support the growing number of Evangelistic teams he sent out. He titled his organization, "The American Christian Workers Union," after it's Irish predecessor. Evangeline and Archie became one of its many teams. At this time, Evangeline wrote to Archie's mother, now widowed and living in Edinburgh, Scotland:

"You asked about the work which we are planning to do... Throughout the Northwest there is much need in rural communities and small villages for the preaching of the gospel. Even in Northern California, we have found many, many places where there is not a service of any kind where one might hear a gospel message. It is to these needy fields we plan to go."

Archie and Evangeline purchased an old trailer and traveled from town to town. Evangeline, experienced in the work and with many helpful contacts, organized their schedules and managed the finances. While the depression raged, Evangeline and Archie found these small rural communities generous supporters. Frequently, the offering consisted entirely of small change. But, between God's provision and Evangeline's careful management, it was always enough.

Much to Evangeline's delight, Archie blossomed in his new ministry. To her, he was a wonderful "people person," a great song leader, and a dynamic preacher. In Stockton, California, only months after launching out on their own, a local pastor told them . "Young man, that was a great message and I believe you have a great future if you will remain faithful."

And remain faithful they did. In town after town, crisscrossing the western United States, the newlyweds brought many to Christ.

Evangeline loved to send and receive mail. And through her correspondence, she developed a strong and loving relationship with Archie's mother. In one letter she wrote, "Last night, Archie gave a most searching message. Then on the other hand, he has a free and easy manner which dispels all prejudice. Our musicals have been quite successful and we seem to be made for each other— that is— in our work, we agree perfectly."

In January of 1937, after a long series of appeals from Archie's Scottish family (many had not yet met Evangeline), the newlyweds began planning a trip to Europe. It would be a homecoming of sorts. Evangeline's father, Walter, Sr., and her brothers Haldane and Walter, Jr. (along with his wife Edith) would accompany them on the voyage. Evangeline and Archie planned to visit his family in England and Scotland. The Duffs would continue on to visit relatives in Ireland.

Planning the trip was difficult. Ship after ship was too full to accommodate the large party. Finally, reservations were made. Evangeline and Archie left their beloved trailer with Helen (who had moved to Oregon), and started out across country by car to New York. Helen had instructions to sell the trailer for Archie and Evangeline. This would clear them of any outstanding debt and give them funds to start anew when they returned from Europe. On May 20, 1937, sailing aboard the Cunard White Star liner, *Berengaria*, they departed for Europe. Archie hoped to spend time in the British Isles holding evangelistic meetings.

As soon as Evangeline and Archie left for Europe, Helen set out to find a buyer for their little trailer. A couple soon agreed to buy it. Helen gave them the title in exchange for their check. But when the couple went to register the trailer, it was discovered that Helen did not have the legal power of attorney needed to complete the sale.

So the sale was delayed. Evangeline and Archie were on board ship somewhere in the mid-Atlantic and could not be reached. They had borrowed money to buy the trailer and the loan repayment date was approaching quickly. Helen was frantic. Suddenly the bank demanded payment in full. On the day payment was past due, the bank repossessed the trailer, sold it to Helen's buyers and kept the full amount of the sale. This left Helen with the job of explaining the bungle to Archie and Evangeline. She was heartsick about the mistake. But, taking pen in hand she wrote:

"I can't help feeling it was my fault, yet I was so helpless. The bank would talk to no one nor make any terms. I surely believe that someone saw a chance to make some money for themselves and did so."

Offering to sell her only car to pay back their losses, Helen closed the letter, "I love you and Archie so much. In my lifetime, I'll find some way of making it up."

This was the disappointing news that greeted Archie and Evangeline when they reached Europe. Of course, they wouldn't consider Helen giving up her car. "But now what?" they asked themselves. The little trailer was their insurance toward the cost of starting over when they returned. $400 meant a great deal to Archie and Evangeline. Feeling the loss greatly, they turned with fervor to the opportunities before them to share the gospel.

Archie's father was the Scottish evangelist, John McNeill. Born in 1854, John McNeill was perhaps one of the most famous preachers of his century. He had pastored churches in Edinburgh, Regents square, London, Liverpool, Toronto, Denver, Alabama, New York and Los Angeles. At each pastorate, his congregations experienced enormous growth. But, even more important was his legacy as an evangelist. Having worked with D.L. Moody, and Charles Spurgeon for more than 16 years, it was not unusual for John McNeill to draw an open air crowd of over 10,000 people. John McNeill, like Evangeline's father Walter Duff, had played an integral part in the extraordinary revival that swept the British Isles at the end of the nineteenth century. His powerful voice, dramatic flair, and delightful sense of humor combined with an almost supernatural understanding of the persons and truths of the Bible, made him extremely popular in both religious and popular circles. He had been active in preaching and evangelism throughout his later years, preaching his last sermon only two weeks before his death in 1933, at the age of 79. Three concurrent memorial services were held in his honor in London, Edinburgh and Glascow.

However, only 30 years after the great revival, the religious climate of Western Europe had grown cold. The pressures of a devastating World War, and ensuing economic prosperity followed by worldwide depression had served to distract most of Europe from her earlier commitment. In only one generation, the British Isles had fallen from faith.

It was to this scene that Archie and Evangeline returned. Yes, they would renew the acquaintances of their youth. Yes, they would visit their families. More importantly, they hoped that by holding meetings, they could return the hearts of their countrymen to God. Would his father's popularity encourage churches to invite Archie and Evangeline to hold meetings? They both hoped it would.

It was a delightful spring for them. They traveled about by train, sight seeing, visiting relatives and, as always, holding whatever meetings could be arranged. Archie had many family connections. His father's first wife had four children before dying suddenly in 1891. John McNeill was remarried in 1898, to Margaret Lee Millar, who gave him six more children. Archie was the youngest son of this second marriage. Remarkably, Margaret had helped the children become a happy, committed family. Thus, the children enjoyed one another and were glad to have this opportunity to spend time together.

Archie, by this time, greatly resembled his father in facial features and stature, though Archie was a good deal taller than John McNeill. Once in Europe, Archie chose to wear a full beard as his father had. Archie's older brother, Cam, put him in his place. "You are not father, Archie, and no amount of looking like him, will make you the great John McNeill."

The beard came off.

While many churches opened their doors to Archie and Evangeline, both the financial and spiritual response of the people was meager. The young McNeills were dependent on the generosity of their audiences to survive. Even staying with relatives, they found it difficult to make ends meet. The European audiences were distracted by the political and social events surrounding them. Food and goods were scarce. Poverty was common.

Most of England was entirely preoccupied by the screaming Fuhrer of Germany. He openly defied England and their own beloved Prime Minister Chamberlain. Hitler stood with his toes on the line of democracy and dared Europe to stop him. Desperate to maintain peace, Chamberlain backed down from every challenge the German leader made. Though hundreds of miles apart, the two leaders exchanged veiled threats and desperate appeasements via the press and the

British Broadcasting Company. With the threat of another war hanging over their every breath, few paused to consider the young American preacher's message.

During this same spring of 1937, Evangeline's mother, Mathilda, was living with her daughter Helen Baugh, on an old farm in Wonder, Oregon. Their large home became the headquarters of the American Christian Workers Union. An older couple served a caretakers for the farm, leaving Helen and Mrs. Duff free to organize and host the evangelistic teams who came and went. As always, Helen organized a large network of prayer support for the Union.

In 1937 the world stood on the brink. There appeared to be only two camps: Those who believed that war was inevitable and those desperate to deny the political danger surrounding Europe and Japan. Noisy isolationists were springing up in the United States as well. Every paper carried editorials and articles cs pousing the wisdom of minding one's own business.

But, there was one petite, brown-eyed, grey-haired Oregon grandmother who was not fooled. She watched the little fuhrer come to power in 1934. She heard him declare the end to the Versailles Treaty in 1935. She watched him re-arm and re-militarize Germany. And She watched as he took the Rhineland in 1936. She knew the English commitment to "non-intervention." But none of these facts alarmed her as much as the news from the Christian press. Even before the secular periodicals published the facts, Mrs. Mathilda Hamilton Duff knew what was coming.

The church in Germany suffered intense persecution at the hand of Hitler. Beginning with regulations to support the NAZI agenda from the pulpit. Soon that was not enough for Hitler. Next he forbade taking offerings. He knew that a church without offerings could not survive. Finally he enforced regulations to proclaim a gospel foreign to the Bible (that Jesus himself was not Jewish). The Christian churches of Germany were then forcibly closed.

But Hitler had not anticipated the tenacity of God's people. Before any other voice of resistance rose in Germany, believers spoke out. They were singled out for destruction. But, their cry was heard by the church in the United States. Mrs. Duff heard it.

Resistant pastors were arrested, beaten and imprisoned. Parishioners were jailed. Persecution of the Jews aroused the conscience of those who belonged to Jesus. As the only group who raised themselves against the Nazi regime, Christians branded themselves to join the persecuted.

The church in the United States noticed. As early as 1936, dire predictions filled the Christian press. One publication quoted a German pastor, "Soon, within not more than 10 or 20 years you Americans will be called upon to face what we are going through."

Mathilda was most alarmed by the persecution of the Jews. The "Christian Century" published the resignation of James G. McDonald, "High Commissioner for the Refugees Coming From Germany." His letter appealed to the League of Nations for intervention in the matter of Jewish persecution in Germany, which he said "...now makes it difficult for these (Jews) to sustain life." In his opinion, the problem had grown in gravity and complexity until it had become a danger to international peace. Intervention was desperately needed.

Mathilda was a woman who knew her Bible. Jewish persecution was something she understood. As the temperature of world politics increased, her prayer for the safety of her husband and children in Europe became more fervent. She was not silent about her fear. "Please consider cutting short your trip" she wrote to Evangeline. "The persecution of the Jews in Germany mounts. I am afraid that we are in for a very dangerous war. Though I don't want to shortchange your work for the Lord, I long for you all to come home."

Walter Sr., Haldane, and Walter Jr. (along with Edith) found conditions in Ireland to be as difficult for the gospel as the McNeills found in England. They agreed to separate, doing their best to cover more territory. But both the crowds and offerings were small. Having no other way to support their work, they too wondered what the Lord had in mind for them.

It was then that Haldane accepted a speaking engagement in Berlin. Certainly he knew the danger. The invitation wasn't much, but it was an opportunity. Surely there was no other place on earth a place where the truth of the gospel was more desperately needed. After some discussion among the family, Haldane agreed to go.

Mathilda wrote frequently to her family. It was no secret that she badly missed them all. She kept track of their comings and goings. They corresponded too—though largely through postcards. When she could, Evangeline was careful to write long descriptions of their trips and meetings. She knew how lonesome her mother was. And, more than the others, Evangeline sensed mother's mounting anxiety about their safety. Evangeline's news came to her regularly, and she was delighted with each arriving card.

Suddenly though, Mathilda sensed something was wrong. She had not heard from Haldane. No one else wrote of him either.

This was because neither the Irish Duffs, nor the Scottish McNeills knew what had happened to him. They too suddenly stopped hearing from Haldane. Prayer was increased on his behalf.

German borders were closed. How would they find him? Before they could start official proceedings to look for him, they received a wire from him requesting money. The elder Duff smiled as he read the wire. Every family expects the youngest to wire for money, he thought. Haldane must be safe.

It wasn't until he returned to Ireland that they discovered Haldane had been arrested and detained in Berlin as a spy. Though his American citizenship protected him, he was changed by the experience. This frightening episode, combined with Mathilda's frequent appeals to return home, convinced the Duffs to sail back to the United States. Just one month later, Archie and Evangeline followed them.

In late November, 1937, the young McNeills crossed the Atlantic for the last time. With what little savings they had left, they purchased a used car in New York City. Gradually, holding meetings along the way, they worked their way to the West Coast.

9

Home Again

$\mathfrak{I}$t was Christmas 1937, before the Duffs were together again at last. Happiest of all was the diminutive grandmother who had prayed her children safely home. "I praise you Lord for your protection of those I love," she prayed. "Praise your wonderful name. You have been so faithful to us. How good to have a Father in heaven who loves us and provides for us and takes care of all our problems."

When the new year of 1938 rolled around, there was one problem still facing Archie and Evangeline. With no trailer, and little savings, they could not travel from town to town along the coast as they had. So, they focused on traveling to villages near Wonder, Oregon. By spring Archie and Evangeline had a new concern. With the anticipation of their first baby, it became apparent that they should consider a more permanent position than that of itinerant evangelist.

They began to look for a pastoral position. Two different Portland, Oregon, congregations expressed a serious interest in Archie's ministry. One was a large successful church with a lovely manse. The other was a church so rundown that the board had only recently decided to try to fill the pulpit rather than disband entirely. Archie and Evangeline committed the question to prayer. Together they decided to let the Lord decide. They would accept the first response they received. In August, their letter of acceptance came from the board of Calvary Presbyterian Church.

The letter, dated August 29, 1838, stated, "This presentation (of Archie's candidacy to the congregation) I am glad to report, was accepted at said meeting without a dissenting vote of any kind." The large successful church requested Archie to become their pastor less than twenty-four hours later.

They began their work in Portland September 1,1938. Immediately they found an apartment just blocks from the church. It was a tiny three room apartment in the back of a large complex. It had no windows, only a series of clerestories above the doors. It wasn't much. But to Evangeline, it was her first opportunity to make a real home, and she settled in with joy.

Calvary Presbyterian was a small congregation, consisting mainly of older persons, with perhaps only 100 members. The building was older still, and was in serious disrepair. It was a congregation struggling to maintain its dwindling numbers.

Located in an area of town bordering on "Goose Hollow," the neighborhood near the church was considered downtown, in an age of migration away from the city. The homes nearby were older. But a great variety of people lived in the neighborhood. Those who were very poor lived next to the stately old homes of the very wealthy. From Archie's first day in the pulpit, it was clear to him that there was very little life left in either the building or the congregation.

Evangeline and Archie began immediately to plan their work. Prayer, they agreed, was their first agenda item, and from the first day they bathed their work with it. Secondly, they agreed that young people were the way to bring life and vitality to this older congregation. Both McNeills had a longstanding love and concern for the unsaved young persons in each community they touched. Their evangelistic hearts found satisfaction in planning ways to reach the young people living in the "Goose Hollow" neighborhood.

This area of Portland's west side was teaming with young people. Heavy drinking and Saturday night carousing made family life miserable for many of the teens. It was not uncommon for children to know only one parent—divorce was rampant. Archie and Evangeline held special meetings for the teens. They scheduled street parades, and street witnessing. They worked. They prayed. And God answered. In a short time, their congregation began to include a vital group of young persons.

In addition, Archie's preaching attracted a select group of young-married couples searching for a church home. Word was circulating in Portland that something exciting was happening at Calvary Presbyterian. Sunday evening services swelled to accommodate those of other congregations who delighted to hear the good preaching of the young Scottish pastor.

Their congregation was growing. But God had plans for Evangeline and Archie to grow as well. During their time at Calvary Presbyterian, a retired missionary from the Christian and Missionary Alliance church lived in Portland. Though nearly 90 and completely blind, Mrs. Harding had begun a ministry to

Portland area pastors. Each Wednesday, she invited them to her home. She challenged them with difficult, intellectual Bible work. "Ministers," she said lovingly, "are a mentally lazy lot. And God cannot use a lazy mind. We must work our mind as we work our body in order to keep it fit for the Master."

To illustrate her point, Mrs. Harding would interrupt her teaching with long multi-step math problems — demanding her listeners solve them without pencil and paper. She stumped the pastors. Before any could answer, the elderly blind woman had the answer herself. She expected of herself what she demanded of them.

Archie and Evangeline never missed an opportunity to be with Mrs. Harding. She challenged them to memorize scripture. This was perhaps her biggest contribution to the young couple. Under her teaching they both strove to successfully memorize large portions of scripture. The work of an old, handicapped woman had influenced their ministry for life.

Another joy was found in Portland. On October 5, 1938, Isabelle Duff McNeill was born. Archie and Evangeline, both in their mid-30s had never experienced such joy. Yes, married life was wonderful. But to Archie, this charming, wonderful, helpless, baby girl was his greatest gift. They were both doting parents. Perhaps Archie was the most delighted father ever to walk the earth. Isabelle accompanied Archie and Evangeline on every outing. She went along to services, speaking engagements, and ministry trips. The youth of Calvary Presbyterian adopted Isabelle as part of their family as well. She was delightfully included whenever she could come along.

Archie and Evangeline were not satisfied with simply bringing the young persons in their community to church. They wanted more. They were after genuine conversions. And still more. They wanted to make disciples. And more. They wanted to give the young people a sense of the importance of ministry. For this reason, Archie often took a team of committed and growing young people to visit any number of locations—jails, hospitals, and unwed-mothers' homes. Archie took them anywhere he felt the gospel was needed. He prepared them for ministry by teaching them to share their faith, and the importance of bathing their ministry efforts in prayer.

Evangeline and Archie took their work very seriously. How many other pastors would march down the aisle of the local theatre to retrieve members of his youthful congregation when movies of questionable content were shown? Archie did. Archie was known to run through neighborhoods chasing boys who avoided his fatherly devotion. But, rather than drive the teenagers away, his devotion and strictness brought them ever nearer. Their number grew.

Unlike other pastors in Portland, Archie kept his home open at all hours. Whether to discuss romantic disappointments or to talk of weighty spiritual matters, there was a constant arrival and departure of young persons needing pastoral attention. Archie and Evangeline also knew that teenagers needed time together, for recreation, as well as relationships. And for this reason, Archie's time at Calvary Presbyterian was punctuated by swimming trips to "Romer's Rest" on the Tualatin River, picnics on Lake Oswego, and camping trips to Driftwood Auto Court located on the Oregon Coast in the tiny village of Cannon Beach.

Archie understood the distractions in the young people's busy lives. So, he and Evangeline came up with an innovative idea. They would take the young people camping for a week. While away, the teens would spend time in recreation together—and have ample opportunity for intensive Bible teaching. Many locations were tried. But, by far the most successful was the Driftwood Auto Park at Cannon Beach, Oregon. Here, Archie and Evangeline took as many as 40 teens at a time. They rented a truck to carry their gear, and persuaded members of their congregation to help with the cooking and chaperoning. After borrowing a trailer for themselves and their daughter, they headed for the coast.

The teens reveled in the attention. They set up their tents, each having it's own name: the "dew-drop" inn, the "just squeeze inn," the "brush inn" and of course, the McNeill's own borrowed trailer was christened the "seldom-inn."

Even in depression days, the week's camping was a bargain. Food, transportation, park rental, plus incidentals were provided for just $4. Though conditions were rough, the "Goose Hollow" kids loved it. The kids ate together on long wooden plank tables. They walked the beach, rode bicycles, and occasionally were fortunate enough to ride horses from the stable across the road. Of course, Archie and Evangeline included morning Bible studies and evening devotions as well.

Archie loved horses. He had taught horseback riding in California, and he delighted to take the children on long rides along the surf. Evangeline loved the

beach as well. She grew to love the sand, the wind, the
ever-changing sky and enormous, endless sea. Of course
Isabelle went along on every trip. She was the thrill of
the teens, drawing endless attention from the girls and
enjoying even the roughhousing of the boys. But besides the play, the sand castles, the campfires and song,
there was also the teaching. It was gentle teaching, full
of love. It was the kind of teaching that lasts a lifetime.

While lives were changing on the beach, the world
was also changing. The United States entered the
Second World War. Archie was overwhelmed by the
desire to speak to the young soldiers going overseas
about their need for Jesus. So, after long days at work,
he would travel to the Portland Serviceman's Center
and speak to lonely, frightened servicemen about the
Captain of the Lord's Army.

Initially a cooperative venture of local Portland
churches, the Servicemen's Center also provided a
wonderful opportunity for the young persons in Archie's
congregation to practice their evangelistic skills. They
often accompanied Archie to the center. Archie was an
evangelist at heart and very successful at bringing
these military men to a decision for Christ. His impos-
ing stature somehow took away the picture of Jesus
being only for the impotent and weak-kneed of society.

Archie was impressed by the closeness of this
work to the work of his father during the First World
War. John McNeill had left an American pastorate to
return to Scotland, where he enlisted with the British
Military as a chaplain. John McNeill brought many
young soldiers to Christ. For the first time, Archie

understood the seriousness that surrounded his father during the war years. Many of these men would never return. Their decisions today were of eternal significance.

As the war dragged on, Archie went day after day to the Service Men's Center. Evangeline hosted dinners for an endless line of young soldiers. Her hospitality provided a connection for young men who were often away from home for the first time. Between her loving concern, and his persuasive witness, many young persons went away ready to meet eternity.

In the late spring of 1940, Evangeline and Archie happily discovered that they were expecting another baby. Isabelle brought such joy to their lives. How wonderful another child would be!

The pregnancy appeared to be progressing normally until one Friday morning in early October. Evangeline had finished her weekly washing and was just picking up in the kitchen when she realized that something was wrong. She called Archie, who quickly took her to the hospital to meet their doctor. The news was not good. At 25 weeks, her "bag of water" had broken. The baby probably would not survive. Their only hope was to hold off labor and delivery.

Evangeline was admitted to the hospital for complete bedrest. It wasn't easy for a woman of her responsibility and energy to lie still. But, she was a model patient. She would do whatever it took to give this baby a fighting chance.

Happily, labor did not occur. One week later it

appeared that the baby was doing well, and Evangeline's condition was stabilized. She was discharged from the hospital with strict orders to continue resting as much as possible.

Then on October 29, Evangeline woke with a fever. She rested all day. However the fever continued. At Archie's urging, she called the doctor. By then labor had begun. Again they went to the hospital.

Though the medical staff tried to stop the labor, the newest McNeill baby was born at 6:55 a.m. the next morning. Archie was with Evangeline at the delivery, and they thankfully named the baby James Duff McNeill. At 29 weeks gestation, he weighed only 3 lbs. 5 oz. He was not well. They began to pray.

The baby lived only two hours and 22 minutes. A short life. But long enough to touch his parents forever. Archie was heartbroken. Evangeline was crushed. When she was able, Evangeline came home to her tiny apartment. It was so empty. Friends cared for Isabelle. Archie went back to work. Evangeline was left to grieve by herself. Her health was badly affected by the delivery. She was anemic and weak. Doctors cared for her blood condition. But she was weak of spirit as well. The tiny congregation did what they could. They cooked meals. They cleaned. They babysat. But only Evangeline could fight the battle that loomed in her spirit. It was a battle of grief. A battle of trust. It was a long and lonely battle. Eventually, the battle was over. The darkness lifted. As Jacob of old, Evangeline struggled with God. She too, came away limping.

In spite of their grief at home, the McNeill's pastorate at Calvary Presbyterian was successful. Under

Archie's hard work both attendance and giving increased. It was enough to make any board happy. But, he also brought with him a faith and creativity that was most unusual. In the second winter of his pastorate, it became apparent that the outside of the old, ornate, steep roofed building needed extensive renovation. The board desired the old style fund raising techniques. But, Archie sent a letter to his congregation. "Rather than engage in lengthy and offensive fund raising," he explained, "we will instead meet for prayer about the matter on the following Wednesday evening. Certainly our Father in heaven knows about our need, and he can supply our need as well." The funds were raised without another word. It was such an unusual approach that it was reported in the Portland daily newspaper.

Archie accepted the Calvary church pastorate without being officially ordained in the Presbyterian church. It was a concern during his candidacy. Was he licensed? Where had he been educated? As they grew to love and respect the work of their dedicated new pastor, the congregation quickly put these questions aside. But Archie never did. As he pastored Calvary Presbyterian, he sought and received his official ordination on April 30, 1943. The congregation had long ago ordained Archie McNeill in love.

In spite of Archie's hard work, the Second World War took its toll on the congregation. Nearly every able-bodied young man left Portland to join the military. Attendance dwindled. At the same time, the numbers of those who were too young to fight grew. The youngsters were sometimes an ill behaved bunch, who tried the patience of the elders and board members.

As church friction increased, Archie's deep commitment to the Service Men's Center had not escaped the notice of its board of directors. The center was growing, and the director needed additional help. It was only natural for the board to invite Archie to join them as the new associate director. It was a difficult decision for Archie. For many of the young men who passed through the center, there would be no other opportunity to make a decision for Christ. This weighed heavily on Archie's thoughts. Yet, he was deeply committed to the ministry of Calvary Presbyterian. He had just celebrated his ordination. It was not so much a matter of which position to choose, as it was a matter of which position to relinquish. He realized that this could be a decision that would change the course of his life.

10

A New Ministry

As with all important decisions, Archie and Evangeline gave this one much attention and prayer. In May of 1943, Archie called a congregational meeting, and read his letter of resignation from the pulpit:

"It is now almost five years ago that your session asked me to supply the pulpit of Calvary Church, and I hardly realize that these years have passed so rapidly. They have been pleasant years for Mrs. McNeill and myself. There have been difficult places, but you have most wonderfully stood by me through them. We have learned to know each other's faults and failings, but as in a human family, these are often easily surmounted by our love for one another and overshadowing (that), our supreme love for Christ. I have prayed earnestly for each of you as you have faced perplexities and troubles. I know you have done the same for me. God has, on many occasions, marvelously answered and so, as we look at our church building today—so beautifully decorated, we feel He alone has all the glory. This is but one of His manifold blessings.

"One of my greatest joys since being here has been the fine group of young men whom God was pleased to send us. Today they are scattered in many parts of the world, fighting for God and country. I pray for them. From time to time they have written me and urged me to do all in my power for the service men— to preach to them, to try to lead them to the Savior. For they realize all too well, a great many will never return.

"About six weeks ago, I was approached by the United Christian Service Men's Center... I had been approached several times before, but had never considered it. Other calls had come from other churches from time to time likewise, but, I was happy in my work at Calvary and felt this was my field. This particular day, God spoke to my heart about it, and it seemed I could not throw it off. I took it to God in prayer. He answered. Today, I feel that God has given me 'marching orders' and I simply asked that this meeting be called to tender my resignation as pastor of this dear church."

Though the McNeills ended their leadership at Calvary Presbyterian, they continued to call it their church home. Having the continued support of old friends helped their transition. The new work with the Service Men's Center also gave them an unexpected blessing. Once again they had time to accept invitations to speak at area churches and events. Archie became a favorite baccalaureate and graduation speaker. He spoke for civic events as well. He spoke for Rotary and Kiwanis. In addition, he was frequently requested as a featured speaker in week-long crusades for youth and adults alike. He would travel as far as California to fulfill the frequent requests. As always, he continued to hold evangelistic services in local congregations. Many Christians in Oregon and Washington

e days of beach camping with the youth of
Presbyterian, she and Archie considered Can-
ch a favorite "get-away." Mathilda was de-
join them. Archie and Evangeline packed up
nd grandmother and headed for the beach.

they were there, Evangeline took a morning
the campground into the tiny village of
each. As she crossed the bridge over Elk
was struck by the incredible beauty of the
n Beach Hotel. There it stood, a large log
two stories, covered with climbing vines.
ds were unkempt, and the grass had been
by the most spectacular display of wild
th the flowers and the vines were in full
sight was so stunning in the morning sun,
line caught her breath. How lovely, she
ntinuing on her way she was struck by the
uld this be it? Is this the property we are
"

ed into the driveway and threaded her
e knee- high grass. The hotel was closed—
for a long time. The building had fallen
disrepair. Still, she carefully edged her
e old porch and peered into the dirty,
ws. Her heart beat faster as she wan-
e porch, from window to window strain-
dimensions of the rooms inside. The
ark. Sizes were difficult to determine.
was a wonderful discovery! She has-
find Archie.

s enjoying his coffee along with the

grew to love the great big preacher with the sweet face
and Scottish accent.

During the McNeill's years at Calvary Presbyterian, Evangeline's sister moved back to San Jose, California. Here, she and her husband Elwood Baugh began a small ministry to Christian professional women.
At first, they held small weekly meetings in local restaurants. Helen Duff Baugh was surprised by the interest in her group. She began to invite speakers from
nearby communities. Her group grew rapidly. Evangeline's
father saw the ministry as having wide-spread potential. He frequently encouraged Helen to plant similar
groups in other cities. After only a short time, Evangeline
and Walter Duff Sr. organized a women's group in
Portland.

Both groups grew with surprising speed. This was
the innocent beginning of the Christian Business and
Professional Women's Council. The San Jose group
soon took on the support of two young women who
brought the gospel message to small villages via summer Bible camps or "After School Clubs." The two
women's councils soon gave birth to councils and missionaries in other cities. Evangeline and Archie opened
their home to the young women missionaries (then
known as Youth Home Missionaries) who were constantly in transit to their various village locations.

The McNeill home in Portland became the over-
night stay, and the unofficial headquarters of this new
Portland organization. An upstairs room was converted
into guest quarters. Archie was always available to
transport the missionaries to and from the bus depot.
Evangeline often visited nearby locations to assist local women in establishing their own groups. She helped

the ladies plan, publicize and carry out their first meetings. Evangeline was available to help in any way—cooking, serving, cleaning up, and was often the featured speaker as well.

Life in Portland during the days of World War II were busy ones for the McNeill family. Archie's work at the Service Men's Center was very successful. There was a constant stream of young soldiers through the McNeill household. But by early 1944, Americans began to dream of victory. The United States made an astronomical investment of men and equipment bound for Europe. Finally hope rose that the end would soon come.

But Archie and Evangeline had more on their minds than the war in Europe, or even the Christian Women's Clubs and Councils. They were beginning to dream a common dream. Having been the featured speaker at many week-long retreats, Archie was struck by the increased attention of his audiences. They were not like Sunday congregations. They seemed focused on the speaker's presentation—more able to respond to the Word of God. There was a freedom for these audiences that was new and wonderful to Archie.

But, there was disappointment in their work as well. Often at a week long conference, many people would make decisions to follow Christ. Unfortunately, when the week was over, Archie would return sadly to Portland realizing how little support the new Christians would find in the small town where he had ministered.

His compelling love of young people rose again to

the surface. He and Evangeli
with the Lord. Then they beg
what if there was a place that
ferences to young people? Co
reach young persons for Chri
maturity and commitment t
possibility seemed enormou
week they envisioned wou
with Bible study, resulting i
To meet these needs, they
cated in a recreational a
dream, it was something t
Gradually, they came to t
might be the leading o
cooperate, they began t
while they continued to

In the spring of th
prayed for eyes to see (
they found beautiful p
that buildings were a p
serious restrictions w
ing materials. This
Evangeline and Arch
was financial. How
director of a Service
sider the purchase

Evangeline's f
conduct evangelis
When he was spe
ence, Evangeline
her family for a

Since th
Calvary
non Bea
lighted t
Isabelle

Whil
walk fro
Cannon
Creek, sh
old Cann
building o
The groun
taken over
flowers. B
bloom. The
that Evang
thought. Co
thought. Co
praying for
She turn
way across th
and had beer
into serious
way across t
paned, wind
dered along t
ing to see th
interior was
Certainly this
tened away to

Archie wa

morning breeze and warm sunshine when he first glimpsed Evangeline hurrying toward him. Her red hair glistened in the sun, and her form was so beautiful he couldn't help but admire his wife as she came closer. Then he became alarmed. She had only just left for town. Why was she back so soon? Her face was flushed. In her hurry, she was out of breath. Still some distance away, she caught his eyes and flashed a radiant smile. Beckoning him, she called, "Come with me Archie— I've found something wonderful." Setting down the cup, he stood up to meet her.

Together they walked the grounds of the old hotel The property possessed many of the qualities they prayed about in a retreat center. Though it was closed, it didn't carry any sign to tell them if indeed it was for sale. "Let's find a real estate man, " Archie suggested. "Certainly he will know if this property is available."

It turned out that finding a Realtor in Cannon Beach was an easy task. There was only one. Yes, he knew about the property. No, it was definitely not for sale. Yes, he knew the owner. In fact, the only Realtor in town, George Frisbee, also happened to be the owner of the old "Cannon Beach Hotel."

As Mr. Frisbee walked Archie and Evangeline from his office to the hotel, he relayed the long and illustrious history of the old building. Around the turn of the century, he said, the first attempt had been made to tow a log cigar raft across the bar at the mouth of the Columbia River. The attempt ended in disaster as the raft broke up in heavy seas. The logs drifted south, and eventually landed on the sand at Cannon Beach.

Mr. George Bill, a Cannon Beach resident, recovered the derelict logs and used them along with other hand hewn lumber to build the charming old building. He managed the building as a hotel during the days of stage coach travel between Astoria and Tillamook.

In those days, the stage traveled south along the coastal beach. This was rugged terrain, following the very narrow old Indian Trail. In areas where the path was too narrow for more than a single coach, the driver often had to stop and give a bellow which echoed along the rock cliffs nearby. If there was no response, he knew the road was clear and he could forge ahead.

In those days there was no bridge at Elk Creek. In order to cross, a wagon usually had to stop and wait for the tide. Sometimes the water was deeper than anticipated, and it came up over the seats of the wagon drenching passengers, baggage and supplies. The route around the narrow rock ledge at Hug Point required the stage and passengers to wait in Cannon Beach for low tide before proceeding south. The Bill's Hotel was the perfect stopping place. Here the passengers enjoyed a good meal and a long rest before they continued their journey.

The hotel was sold in 1913 to Edna Osborne, who changed the name to the Cannon Beach Hotel, and continued its successful operation. She, along with her parents, developed the inn's reputation of extraordinary dining. Under her management, the hotel was visited by some of Oregon's finest families along with President Woodrow Wilson and William Jennings Bryan. Edna eventually married George Frisbee, and together they ran the hotel for the next few years. During the First World War however, the building was needed by the Coast Guard who housed over 100 men there. Since then it had not been used or cared for, Mr. Frisbee reported. No, it was not for sale, he repeated. But, should they decide to sell in the future, they would only consider a cash offer.

Disappointed, Evangeline and Archie toured the old log building anyway. Approaching the front door from the west they crossed a wide covered sitting porch. The main entrance was a heavy wooden door held by a huge ship's lock. The door was framed by tiny window panes now nearly covered by vines and profuse shrubbery. Inside, they discovered a huge 30-by-50 foot lounge, punctuated at its southwest end by a massive fireplace.

The fireplace dominated the room. It was constructed of smooth round river rock with a fire box about 42 inches wide and three feet high. The box was arched on top and the stones extended to the ceiling of the room.

In the opposite corner, stood an attached "lean to" kitchen area for the preparation of the meals. The huge room served as both a dining area and lounge.

The logs which made up the building were not uniform in size, nor had they been peeled before they were notched and set in place. There was no paint or plaster, but only dark wooden walls surrounding the space. At the northerly end of the great room, a narrow staircase led to a small landing then turned and proceeded to the second floor.

Upstairs, a narrow hallway ran the length of the center of the building. Here, Archie and Evangeline found 10 large bedrooms, five facing the vista of the sea, and five overlooking the beautiful coastal mountains. At the end of the hall were somewhat rustic bathroom facilities. The entire building was heated by the single-stone fireplace downstairs.

Returning again downstairs to the main room, Mr. Frisbee asked Archie and Evangeline about their plans for the old rundown building. With great excitement, Archie explained his dream of a youth camp and conference center. Mr. Frisbee listened attentively, and though he seemed pleased with the thought of using the building for this purpose, he was adamant about his terms. He would only consider cash.

Graciously, the Realtor and pastor parted company. Mr. Frisbee headed for his office in the village, while Archie and Evangeline returned to their campground. "The place is perfect," Evangeline exclaimed, "great location, good size, such potential—well not truly perfect. But, we have the vision, the energy, the dream—it could be perfect ..." But for one insurmountable problem. Cash.

Together, Archie and Evangeline schemed. How could they make the property their own? During the rest of their vacation, they often returned to the property. Sometimes they met Mr. Frisbee there. He continued to be gracious, but unwavering in his demand for a cash sale. Many times they returned alone—to plan, to dream, to pray. It was with sadness that, when their vacation was over, they returned to the city and their home.

Back in Portland, Archie and Evangeline continued to make the Cannon Beach site the subject of much prayer. After several weeks, they decided to meet Mr. Frisbee at the hotel one last time. On the chosen day, fall was in the air. The vine maple was in its brilliant fall dress. It was a beautiful day for a drive to the ocean. There was an unexplainable lightness in the heart of Archie and Evangeline. Could this be the day that would make the old hotel their own?

Once again Mr. Frisbee let them in the grand old door. Once again they toured the upstairs bedrooms. At last they stood chatting by the fireplace. Mr. Frisbee had not changed his mind. He wanted cash—more cash than any preacher could readily obtain. While they visited, a pickup truck drove into the driveway. Excusing himself, Mr. Frisbee said, "This man also wants to purchase the property," and he headed out to greet the visitor.

With heavy hearts, both Archie and Evangeline knew it was time to pray. Together, they knelt on the old fireplace hearth. Archie began, "Lord, we do not want this property for our own use. We only want it for Thy Glory. We cannot purchase it for cash. But Lord, it is nothing for you to change this man's heart." And from memory, Archie reminded God of His own Words, "'The king's heart is in the hand of the Lord, as rivers of water; He turneth it whithersoever He will.' Now Lord, if you want us to have it, it is nothing for you to change Mr. Frisbee's heart."

When Mr. Frisbee returned, he said nothing of what transpired on the driveway. "I will see you in Portland one of these days," Mr. Frisbee said in an awkward good-by. So Archie and Evangeline, without any real answers, made the long and silent trip back to Portland.

The McNeills led busy lives. When they returned

to Portland, they immediately went back to work. They were scheduled to hold a series of city wide meetings further east, on the Columbia River, near The Dalles, Oregon. Archie and Evangeline were unsure of the meaning in Mr. Frisbee's last comment. So, they proceeded to The Dalles.

Near The Dalles, Archie and Evangeline stayed with friends who were members of the host church. One warm afternoon, their host, Mrs. Brickwedell, answered the phone to a Mr. Frisbee, from Cannon Beach. He traced Archie and Evangeline all the way to The Dalles to offer them the property exactly according to their terms.

There was much celebration that night in the Brickwedell home. Everyone knew that only God could have accomplished what they witnessed. It was a celebration of joy, of praise, and of immense gratitude.

When finally they met to sign the real estate contract, Mr. Frisbee reminded them of their last meeting at the old hotel. "Did you ever wonder what happened when I went out to greet the driver of the pickup truck on the driveway?" he asked. "Well, the man in the truck handed me payment in full for the price of the property. I took the payment, but somehow—I don't know how to explain this— I didn't want the money. I wanted you folks to have the property. So, I told him, 'I'm sorry, the property has just been sold.'"

And so, on September 23, 1944, Archie and Evangeline McNeill signed a contract for the purchase of seven acres, a hotel building, and several outbuildings located in the tiny village of Cannon Beach, Oregon. For

Archie and Evangeline, more happened that day than simply signing real estate papers. Mr. Frisbee's little story was the confirmation of new "marching orders" from God. This was tangible evidence that God had indeed led them into a new ministry.

The war was nearly over. It was only a matter of time before the flow of young soldiers into Portland ended. The Service Men's Center would close and Archie would be free to follow this new lead. There was no longer any doubt. This was God's new task. This was His new purpose for the two of them. Archie and Evangeline, each with all their heart and all their worldly goods, made a commitment that day to pursue this new direction from God.

How He would lead, how He would accomplish the task was still to be seen. But no one could take away the peace of heart that came that day, in knowing His divine direction—in seeing His perfect stamp of provision for the dream they dared to dream together.

Pictorial

Rev. Archie McNeil in 1951

Evangeline Duff (McNeill) with concert harp in 1920s

B

The Duff Family in International Falls, Minnesota, after the birth of Baby Haldane. From left, first row: Walter, Sr., Haldane. Second row: Olive, Walter, Jr., (Alexandria) Evangeline. Back row: Helen, Matilda.

C

Evangeline and her brother Walter in the 1920s with the Duff family touring car.

The Duff Sisters Trio
From left to right: Evangeline, Helen and Olive

D

Evangeline and sister Helen with a "motorhome" about 1918

E

Evangeline in 1930s

F

Archie and Evangeline, wedding photo, 1936

The old Bill Hotel, the original site of the Cannon Beach Conference Center, in the summer of 1945

H

Above: **The first Chapel** *of the Conference Center is on right, cabins on left*

Left: Evangeline and Archie, summer 1949

I

The first summer guests at the Conference Center, July 1945

J

Archie and Evangeline with daughter Heather (Isabel) and "Snooper," 1945

K

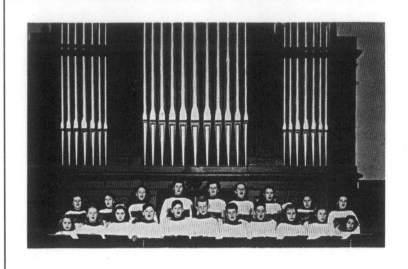

Calvary
Presbyterian Church

S. W. 11th and Clay Streets

"Fear not ye: for I know that ye seek Jesus, which was crucified.
He is not here; for he is risen, as he said."   - -Matthew 28:5, 6.

*Calvary Presbyterian Church in Portland, Archie
McNeil listed in program as Pastor in 1943*

L

Morning Services

11:00 A. M.

PRELUDE Hymn of Glory..Pietro A. Yon

PROCESSIONAL -Christ the Lord is Risen Today................Charles Wesley

DOXOLOGY

APOSTLES CREED

GLORIA PATRI

INVOCATION

Vibra Harp Solo Selected.. Mrs. A. McNeill

HYMN Christ the Lord is Risen Today...Page 98

RESPONSIVE READING ....Selection 500

CHOIR ANTHEM Lo! He Comes ....Sicilian Mariners' Hymn
                              Children's Choir

PRAYER

Trumpet Solo Christ Arose..Robert Lowry
                              Wesley Aplanalp

HYMN When I survey the Wondrous Cross....................................Page 88

OFFERTORY Easter-Dawn ....Aloys Claussmann
    "As it began to dawn, toward the first day of the week, came Mary
    Magdalene and the other Mary to see the Sepulcher."
                                                    St. Matthew 28.

SERMON "Who is this King of Glory"..................................Archie McNeill

PRAYER

ORGAN -Hallelujah Chorus..Handel

BENEDICTION

POSTLUDE Easter Alleluia..Aloys Ottenwaldor
                    "Now is Christ risen from the dead"

Calvary Presbyterian Church, Order of Service listed in 1943 program

M

Evening Services

5:30 P. M.

PRELUDE   "All Glory be to God on High"......................Garth Edmundson

HYMN   Hark! Ten Thousand Harps and Voices.. ....Page 10?

INVOCATION

SCRIPTURE

CHOIR ANTHEM   There is a Green Hill Far Away........ ....G. Stebbins
Children's Choir

PRAYER

OFFERTORY   Fountain Reverie...P. E. Fletcher

SERMON   "Where Have They Laid Him"........................Archie McNeil.

POSTLUDE   Hosannah!..J. P. E. Hartmann

N

Calvary Presbyterian Church

S. W. 11th Avenue and Clay

PORTLAND, OREGON

ARCHIE McNEIL,
Pastor

VICTORIA APLANALP
Organist and Choir Director

Clerk of Session	Secretary	Treasurer
R. E. Dodd	T. P. Thoresen	G. G. Muirden
2038 S. W. 6th Ave.	1508 S. W. Market	629 S. W. Market

BIBLE SCHOOL Meets every Sunday morning at 9:45 a.m.
Graded classes for ALL ages

Regular Church Services

MORNING SERVICES: Every Sunday....................................11:00 a.m

EVENING SERVICES: Every Sunday.....................................

PRAYER MEETINGS: Every Wednesday............................ 7:30 p.m

BIBLE SCHOOL: Every Sunday.. 9:45 a.m

OUR CHURCH

Incorporated June 23rd, 1880, 63 years ago
Organized February 20th, 1882, 61 years ago

The first service was held October 9th, 1883, nearly sixty years
ago, and services have been held continuously since that time.

The 25th anniversary celebration was held on April 15th, 1907.

Back cover of program used by Portland's Calvary Presbyterian Church in 1943

O

Don't Miss A Minute...

Evangeline & Archie **McNeill**

~~~~~*Scotch - Irish Duo*~~~~~

March 9 - 16

"HE'S SCOTCH" . . Born in Kilmalcoln, Scotland and son of the noted Scottish Preacher, the Rev. John McNeill. A fluent speaker and Bible Expositor. Director of Cannon Beach Bible Conference, & West Coast Rep. of Village Missions.

"SHE'S IRISH" . . . **Vibraharpist** . . . formerly a member of the DUFF IRISH TRIO. Sings quaint Irish airs, hymns, and Negro spirituals. Born in Londonderry, Ireland.

COMMUNITY

Presbyterian Church

BOARDMAN, OREGON   **8:00 EACH NIGHT EXCEPT SATURDAY**

Flier for program provided by Evangeline and Archie

P

Archie and Evangeline with instruments in 1940s

Q

Portland Minister Dies in Crash
While Returning to Cannon Beach

CANNON BEACH, Aug. 6.— The Rev. Archie McNeill, 46, of Portland and Cannon Beach, was instantly killed in an auto-truck crash on the Sunset highway three miles east of Timber junction late Tuesday.

State police, who investigated, said the minister apparently was blinded by the sun about 4:45 p. m., and was on the wrong side of the road when his car struck the truck driven by Alex Getz, 8054 SE 9th avenue, Portland. The truck was overturned, but Getz was uninjured.

The Rev. Mr. McNeill, headed west, was returning from Portland, where he had purchased supplies

Rev. Archie McNeill

for the Cannon Beach Bible conference grounds, of which he was owner and director. The groceries were strewn on the highway, and traffic was blocked briefly.

Getz, driver for the Porter W. Yett Construction company, is working on a resurfacing job on the Quartz creek bridge section of the highway.

The minister's body was taken to the Tillamook county morgue by Allen E. Lundberg, coroner.

The crash victim was born in Scotland. He is survived by his wife, Evangeline; daughters, Isabel, 14, and Helen Jean, 4; his mother, Mrs. Margaret McNeill, in England; a brother in South Africa, and half-sisters, one in Scotland and another in England.

Obituary
August 6, 1952

R

Evangeline's Family, 1957. From left: Haldane, Evangeline, Helen, Mother Duff, Olive, Walter, Jr.

Evangeline with Judy Hayne and Dorothy Ball, staff members during the 1950s and early 1960s.

S

Evangeline, late 1950s

Evangeline with her first grandchild, Andrew Steynor, 1975

T

Evangeline in the 1970s

U

11

The First Summer

Cannon Beach Bible Conference. That was the new baby's name. Soon, everyone in Evangeline's family was excited about the progress and growth of the plans. Archie and Evangeline took possession of the property during the Christmas season. But the dreary wet weather of an Oregon winter could not dampen their anticipation. The family often gathered down at the beach to clean up the old hotel. There were furnishings to find, a kitchen to establish, weeds to remove, flowers to plant.

Slowly the old hotel took on its new look. The four small cabins would be family guest rooms. The old officer's quarters ("The Annex") would be the deluxe accommodations (the rooms had sinks!). The log hotel had 10 rooms upstairs, with bathrooms located at the end of the hallway. Together it was enough for a start. The main floor of the log lodge was large enough to house both the dining area and space for the main meeting. It would work. The dream was becoming reality.

Winter of 1945 was a time of hope. The century's second great war appeared to be coming to an end. Evangeline and Archie looked forward to the end of the conflict as well. But, they worried about the effect returning soldiers would have on the U.S. economy. Would the influx of unemployed men cause the value of the dollar to fall? They saved every nickel in an effort to pay off the conference center property.

Forming a board of directors, they established the non-profit status of the ministry. While the land and building were privately owned by the McNeills, the corporation made plans to purchase the property as soon as the funds became available. The next important step was to write their statement of purpose. With much prayer, they asked the Lord, "What is your plan for our ministry? What do you wish to accomplish here?" In time, they chose these words:

"Cannon Beach Christian Conference Center is interdenominational and works with the Church-at-large. Its presents the Word of God in its entirety and its simplicity. It challenges Christians to consistent Christian living, thus strengthening the spiritual life of the Church-at-large. It stresses the Word of God, the walk with God, witnessing and missions."

As the McNeills continued their evangelism campaigns in local churches, they introduced this new ministry. They solicited both financial and physical help. A small lumber mill in central Oregon was the first to donate materials for structural repairs. Archie, Walter, and Haldane spent hours repairing the buildings. The years of Coast Guard use had been hard on the all the structures. There were windows to replace, roofs that leaked and large holes in interior walls. They began the back breaking work of jacking up the log cabin in order to replace the lower logs, rotten from contact with the damp soil at the base of the building. They planned heating and lighting for the buildings. Archie had little experience with the practicalities of renovation. But Evangeline's brother, Walter Duff, Jr., was never without a clever and cost-saving solution to the latest problem. The men pounded and the ladies painted. Together, the repair team moved toward the opening of the season.

Evangeline planned the summer schedule. They would open on the 16th of July, 1945. This, they hoped, would avoid the uncertain spring weather of the Oregon coast. They planned four, one-week conferences. The first and the third weeks would be especially for the women of the Christian Business and Professional Women's Clubs and Councils. Room and board for a one-week conference would total $16.50. Evangeline was in charge of advertising the conference center. Here, her years with the Duff Gospel Trio came in handy. She designed and printed modest brochures which went with them wherever she and Archie traveled to speak.

It was imperative that the cost of operating the ministry be kept to an absolute minimum. So, Evangeline recruited volunteer help to provide guest services. She found people to cook and serve meals. She found others to do dishes and clean rooms. She invited a friend to operate the reception desk. She found someone to maintain the books and receive donations. She found persons to help with ground maintenances. These were people she knew, people who were interested in the ministry. They were people who were willing to invest themselves in an opportunity to share the truth of the gospel with others. Some were relatives. Some were friends. Some were former church members, or young people. Some she met as she traveled for the Christian Business and Professional Women's Clubs and Councils.

As winter turned to spring, every weekend found some group of people at Cannon Beach readying the buildings for the big July opening. With the end of the war in sight, Archie resigned from the Service Men's Center and the McNeills made their permanent home on the conference grounds.

At last, they were ready for the opening. With much excitement, Archie and Evangeline received the very first registration by mail. Someone wanted to come spend a week at their retreat by the ocean!

That first summer was a delightful success. All four conference weeks were satisfactorily filled. Archie and Evangeline worked hard to make their guests feel as though they were visiting a private home rather than a conference grounds. They hosted picnics at Ecola Park. Archie taught his guests to ride horses on the beach. Evangeline took others on scenic hikes. They welcomed conference visitors personally and often walked them to their car to say good-bye.

The short four-week season had been exhausting. Not only did Archie and Evangeline serve as host and hostess, but they also cleaned, cooked, shopped for groceries, paid bills, washed laundry, and cared for their own family. Whatever was not be done by the volunteers was done by the McNeills.

It was the wonderful exhaustion of success. Never were they more sure of God's new direction for their lives. Guests left excited and grateful for their week at the beach. And, after the season closed, Evangeline and Archie were overwhelmed when two men approached them with a suggestion for expansion.

"This Conference Center is a wonderful gift of God. It must grow," they said. "You need to build a dining hall that is large enough to prepare and serve many more guests. If you can get the materials, we will help you build the building."

This was exciting confirmation for Archie and Evangeline. However, the monthly property payment of $200 was already a struggle. How could they afford an additional building? One of the men, a builder, agreed to draw up the lumber order. Archie and Evangeline agreed to ask a supplier if he would sell the lumber wholesale.

They went to visit Mr. Ben Ellis, a lumberman, in his Corvallis home. While they eagerly explained their mission, he listened attentively. After looking at their lumber order, the lumberman handed the sheet of paper to his wife. She read it slowly and returned the sheet without a word. The silence grew heavy. Finally, Mr. Ellis spoke, "My wife and I would like to donate the entire lumber order as a gift."

This was more than Archie and Evangeline had ever imagined. They were ecstatic with the news. They thanked Mr. Ellis prolifically, and with much enthusiasm returned to the coast. How faithful God was to their needs!

Soon after, God's faithfulness was put to the test again. In January, Archie ordered a large collection of peeler logs from a local paper mill. He was praying that the sale of his Portland home would provide the funds to pay for them. The wood was cheap and sturdy. The plan was to use the peeler logs as exterior lumber for the new dining hall. The mill would contact them once the half logs became available.

About this time, the buyer of their Portland home began defaulting on his monthly payments. Archie and Evangeline didn't have any extra money. They began to hope the mills wouldn't find the logs they needed. Then the call came. The logs were ready. They would need to pay for them at the time of delivery.

Their hearts were heavy with worry, until the next day in prayer, Evangeline had a verse of scripture come alive for her. "My God shall supply all your needs according to his riches in glory." With tears, she showed the verse to Archie.

The next day they went to Portland to see the buyer of their house. The buyer greeted them with a pleasant welcome, saying, "Mr. McNeill, I want to consolidate my obligations. The full amount due you on the house will be in your hands tomorrow." As they drove back to the coast, they realized—the amount due on the contract was exactly the amount needed to clear the bill on the half logs!

Archie continued to speak, traveling from church to church. Everywhere he spoke about his vision for the conference center. Whenever possible, Evangeline and Isabelle traveled with him.

They planned a work party for the spring of 1946. A fair sized group of men joined Archie, Evangeline and the two men who spearheaded the dining hall idea. Evangeline cooked. Archie and the men built. When they were ready for the roof, they prayed together for clear weather. It was a bold request for

March on the Oregon Coast. The day dawned with summerlike sunshine. The roof was completed.

The next summer, the conference center season opened with a brand new two-story dining hall. The upper floor housed two large dormitory areas. The main floor of the 40-by-80 building housed the kitchen and dining room and a small reception area. The building was named Ecola.

The "Work Week" crew for the spring of 1947 found themselves building a new chapel building, also of peeler logs. The number of guest weeks increased as did attendance. The McNeills were constantly trying to stay ahead of their growing ministry. They established a mailing list of conference friends. They moved the small Coast Guard buildings to the back of the property and built another small guest building. To their delight, other church groups began to request the conference center as a location for private retreats. These were easily accommodated in non-conference weeks. Any small increase in income helped to defray the center's overhead. The McNeills began to hire help. They added a caretaker, and a summer cook. Gradually, the volunteer help was supported by a small staff of paid help. Still, Archie and Evangeline worked tirelessly to keep the small operation going.

As they struggled to provide new space for the growth they experienced, the old buildings demanded care and attention. They were in need of constant repair. New foundations here. New floors there.

They discovered, to their surprise, that the new living space over the dining room had at least one serious drawback. When people walked upstairs during dinner, the sand caked to their shoes came sifting down through the single layer floor onto the dinner tables below. People came to the conference center to enjoy the beach—but not in their food! Another layer of flooring was quickly added above the dining room.

Though the conference center required enormous amounts of energy, Archie and Evangeline found it very satisfying. This was their place. This was their calling. Archie, with his charming public manner, was the ideal conference director. Evangeline, with her ability to plan and oversee the conference details, was his perfect complement. Together they seemed ideally chosen for this exciting, though exhausting ministry. Everyone who knew them agreed. Surely God brought this pair together for this purpose. What great things they could accomplish!

12

Alone

"**M**ISSIONARY." Evangeline clearly printed these capital letters in the space labeled "occupation." She smiled as she looked at the word. It took her a great deal of time to come to this decision. Such a small thing—naming your occupation. But it was not a small thing to Evangeline. This was the first income-tax form she would file without Archie's help.

Over the past eight months, she found herself wrestling with her new role. What was she? Conference Director? Evangelist? Pastor? Women's Club Or ganizer? Words were important to Evangeline. What was the right word for her new role in life? Missionary seemed to say it all. Of this one thing she was sure, her life's purpose was to bring people in her world to the Savior.

Missionary. Yes. That seemed to say it. The date was April 15, 1953. She would have to hurry to get the forms finished and into the mail. Many of spaces on this year's form held new information. It was a year of much change for Evangeline. The space where last year she printed "married," now held the word "widowed." Where last year she wrote Archie's name, this year she simply wrote, "deceased." Who would think so much pain could be found filling out an income-tax form?

But more than labels changed since last year. The woman returning to the Oregon Coast in the spring of 1953, was different as well. She was a stronger woman. A determined woman. She knew the leading of God in her life. He had, unmistakably, led her to this point. To this place. Under these conditions. She would not give up. She would not surrender. She had a strong Christian heritage. Her family stood ready to help at a moment's notice. Two brothers were nearby. Haldane held a pastorate in Seattle and Walter lived in Dallas, Oregon.

The summer conference schedule was planned in Kansas. Helen's staff helped Evangeline prepare and mail the advertisements and brochures. Now that she was back in Cannon Beach, there was nothing left to do but carry out the season. With faith and determination, she went to work.

It was not long into that first season without Archie that Evangeline began to make some striking discoveries. She was not the only one who carried treasured memories of Archie. He had touched people everywhere, in all walks of life. He was alive in their memories. Since his death, Evangeline received more than 1,500 messages of condolences. These people, who cared about Archie, now cared about the ministry of the conference center. It represented a way for people who loved Archie, to act out their love. These people came from everywhere. They volunteered to put an addition on the chapel in his memory. They donated money to the ministry. They gave of their time and talents and resources. Whatever was needed, they gave.

Certainly, Evangeline continued to grieve. Everything in Cannon Beach seemed to remind her that he was gone. Here was his favorite chair. There was someone riding horses on the beach the way they had ridden. She missed him terribly. When he was alive, they made conference center decisions together. Now, she had to think through problems alone. She missed his practical approach to life.

But during this first season alone, Evangeline also discovered something even more remarkable. In the Bible, she found new significance in the promise that God would be a "father to the fatherless, a defender of widows." (Psalms 68:5) She felt new confidence in waiting for the Lord's solutions to her problems. Her reasoning was simple. "If God chose to put me in this place of leadership alone, then I can depend on Him to meet my every need."

Her course of action reflected this simple philosophy. She made every detail a matter of genuine, earnest prayer. It did not matter to her whether the need was great or small. She prayed over everything. Then, as soon as she lifted her head from prayer, she began to look for His answer. To Evangeline, God could be depended upon for anything from parking places to lumber, groceries to refrigerators. It wasn't as if Evangeline had another source. God was her source. And He would use whatever means He chose to provide for her. Her only joy was to watch and see how He would bring His answers to pass.

With each answer to prayer, her confidence grew. She began to see how God used people to meet her needs. All kinds of people. Some were Christians. Many were not. She began to have the courage to make her needs known to both Christians and non-Christians alike. Men came and built what came to be called the Administration building. It was constructed from the torn-down school building's lumber. Here, on the main floor, she located her office. Every day as she unlocked the door to her office, she was reminded of God's unfailing provision of materials and labor. It gave her the courage to keep going.

Perhaps this extraordinary support would ebb as the memory of Archie dimmed. Evangeline decided to enjoy it for as long as it might last.

The support continued, and attendance at the conference center increased. Evangeline continued to return every winter to the headquarters of the Christian Women's Clubs and Councils in Missouri, where she planned the summer conference schedule. Every spring she returned to the coast to supervise the summer conferences.

By the summer of 1956, two weeks of youth camps were added to the conference schedule. One week was for junior-high children, the other was for high-school youth. These two weeks were very well attended, with more than three hundred teens at each camp. In one case, two carloads of children were driven out from Colorado to attend. Evangeline hired a local pastor to serve as director. She also chose a dynamic speaker for the young people, while her own staff planned the activities and provided for the camper's physical needs. Many young people came to know Christ.

The success of the youth camps brought a new problem to Evangeline's attention. Weather on the Oregon coast was not predictable enough to plan on entertaining 300 teenagers outside. She felt that the conference center needed a large recreational type building to house youth activities. With that in mind, she set out to build a gymnasium.

As usual, the biggest obstacle to a building project was obtaining the needed materials. Evangeline had volunteer help, but she could not afford building supplies. Bankers, she discovered, would not consider loans to the conference center. On one such inquiry, the banker told her, "We don't lend to 'fly by night' nonprofit organizations." She determined never again to ask for a loan.

Several conference friends encouraged her to contact yet another lumberman in Portland. Evangeline was hesitant to ask a complete stranger for help. Still, she bathed the suggestion in prayer. Finally, she arranged to call him at his mill. When the call went through, Mr. George Miller was not at the office. She called him at home. He seemed very gruff when he asked, "What do you want?"

Carefully, Evangeline explained the work of the conference center and her need to purchase a great deal of lumber to build a new gym. She closed with the request to purchase the lumber wholesale. Mr. Miller answered her abruptly, "Who are you?" And without waiting for a reply, he went on, "Are you Archie McNeill's wife?"

Mrs. McNeill responded positively.

He went on, "And are you Reverend Walter Duff's daughter?"

Again, Evangeline said that she was.

"Send me the lumber order by mail. It is your's."

With the lumber gift in hand, Evangeline asked for volunteer help to build the gym. On Sunday July 22,

1956, she and the conference center friends dedicated the new 100-by-56-foot building which housed a 40-by-80-foot gym, a lounge and restrooms. The gym was from the Lord; Evangeline was sure. But those men who helped her build it were delighted to discover that Evangeline could handle a hammer as well as anyone. She prayed. She asked for help. And, she helped nail the floor boards of the gym in place herself.

Those who worked with Evangeline, soon learned that there was no job she would not do. She painted. She cooked. She cleaned toilets. The kitchen staff was never surprised to have her drop by to peel potatoes with them. Then she would give some bit of advice to the cook and be off to other responsibilities.

In spite of Archie's absence, Evangeline's work brought deep satisfaction to her. Her energy level seemed to multiply with every expansion of the conference center facilities. She had a few people she could count on to help her through. She depended heavily on them. Her bookkeeper helped her manage financial details. She had great trust in her handyman and a carpenter friend of the conference center. She also found a designer who drew plans for the buildings she envisioned. These men answered her call for help again and again. Together, they were a team that made the conference center a growing reality.

While Evangeline supervised the growing conference center ministry, she did her best to raise her two girls. Her mother was there to help. But, without Archie, it was not an easy task. Isabelle, now in her mid-teens was growing more unhappy with her given name. "I hate my name, mother," she cried. "The kids make such horrible nicknames out of it. I want to choose a new name."

Evangeline understood the pain of awkward nick-names. She lived through the same misery. The little family agreed it was time to listen carefully for a new name for Isabelle.

It was little Helen Jean who, in the second grade, came up with the solution. One day she arrived home from school, bounced into the kitchen and announced that she had found the perfect name for her big sister. "There is a new girl in my class," she confided, "and her name is Heather. Isn't that the most beautiful name? I think that we should change Isabelle's name to Heather."

Isabelle agreed that the name was perfect. But she wondered how to accomplish the name change. Evangeline had the answer. The next time they enrolled Isabelle in a new school, they would register her as Heather. Since they changed schools twice each year, it would be no problem. Isabelle Duff McNeill became Heather Duff McNeill.

The next year again brought sorrow to Evangeline. In March of 1957, her mother, Mathilda Hamilton Duff, passed away. Mathilda spent many of her last years with Evangeline. She helped Evangeline through the great loss of Archie. Together, year after year, they made the trip back and forth to Stonecroft in Missouri. Mathilda supervised the children while Evangeline did her traveling for Christian Women's Clubs and

Councils. Her death was a great personal loss to Evangeline.

Haldane, Evangeline's younger brother, recognized her sorrow and arranged to spend a few days with her after the funeral. Together they took long hikes on the beach, visiting, and remembering. Returning one day from the beach, they passed the ramshackle remains of the Cannon Beach Recreation Center. Haldane paused. It was as if he had never seen the building before.

"You know, Evangeline," he said, "You should buy this property for the conference center. What a beautiful location! Right on the oceanfront—It is just a block from the grounds... Perhaps a dining hall....The view is breathtaking!"

That was all he said. But Evangeline long believed such innocent comments—a passing suggestion, a phrase dropped inadvertently—were often God's way of speaking to her. She began to bring the idea to the Lord in prayer. "Is this from you Lord? Please let me know."

The idea would not leave her mind. She began to investigate the property. She found that the owner happened to be spending the winter in Cannon Beach. She called him and made an appointment to see the building.

Mr. Mahon was very happy to show her the property. As they passed through the building, he told Evangeline how this could be altered or that could be fixed.

Evangeline was thinking. How does one wreck a building?

Unfortunately, Mr. Mahon did not have all the building keys with him. So they agreed to meet again the next day to view the rest of the property. As they parted, Mr. Mahon told Evangeline, "For only $20,000, you can have the four lots, the swimming pool and the buildings."

Evangeline spent a troubled night. To her, the pool was a rusted out safety hazard. The building needed to be demolished. And, of course, there was the small issue of money. She didn't have $20,000. For that matter, she didn't have $200. "Lord," she prayed, "is this your arrangement or mine?"

Then the thought came to her. "Offer him $15,000 cash. If he agrees to the twenty five percent reduction in price, you will know the property is from me." This settled her course of action. In peace, she slept through the rest of the night.

The next day, she met Mr. Mahon at the appointed hour. He drove her to the property. As he was unlocking the door, she said, "Mr. Mahon, before we look further, I just wanted you to know what happened last night. I prayed about this and I am going to offer you $15,000 cash. If you accept, then I know God wants us to have the property. If you don't take the offer, there will be no hard feelings. I will know it is not for us."

With that he snapped the lock closed. Evangeline thought perhaps he was very angry. "I'll walk home," she said quietly.

"No, no, get into the car," he replied.

He did not speak until they were back to the conference center. "Mrs. McNeill, what did you say to me?"

She repeated her offer.

"Well, I don't own the property myself. My wife and mother-in-law also have an interest. I will talk with them." With that, he drove away.

Evangeline was quite convinced she would never hear from him again. So she was surprised, an hour later, to answer his knock at her front door. She invited him in. Her surprise turned to amazement when he told her that the family had agreed to her offer. "I'm on my way to Portland right now to see our attorney," he told her.

As she closed the door behind him, Evangeline stood in a state of shock. "Father, what do we do now?" The conference center had not a penny in the bank for purchase of additional land. At least now, she had confirmation of the Lord's leading. The Lord would just have to provide the funds as well.

When Archie died in 1952, some friends told Evangeline they would be glad to loan her money if she should ever have the need. In the past, she borrowed a small amount occasionally to get the summer season started. She wondered if perhaps these people would consider another loan for the purchase of property. The next morning she drove to visit them in Corvallis, Oregon.

"Mrs. McNeill, you know I would be glad to loan you the money. But I don't have any to loan at this minute. A man owes me $5,000. But, he has even defaulted on the interest payments. There is little hope in that."

Disappointed, Evangeline stood to leave.

"Let's pray before you go," her friend suggested.

As she put on her coat, her friend said, "You know, Evangeline, I think I'll go speak with the man who owes me money."

Evangeline returned to Cannon Beach via Portland where she stopped to visit another friend who might be able to help. This friend was away on vacation. What could she do? She headed for the coast.

When she arrived, her Corvallis friend called her on the phone. "You will never believe what happened," he said. "I went to see the man who owes me money, and without an explanation, he gave me a check for the entire $5,000. It had to be an answer to our prayer. The check is in the mail. It should be in Cannon Beach by tomorrow."

Evangeline was grateful. This was certainly an answer to prayer. But $5,000, no matter how miraculous, was not $15,000. Where would she find the additional $10,000? She spent the rest of the evening thanking and praising the Lord for His miracle. At the same time she asked. "What next?"

Early the next morning, Mr. Mahon returned to visit Evangeline. She could see that he was agitated. It wasn't long before he came out with it. "Mrs. McNeill," he began, "My attorney tells me I cannot sell that property for cash. All I can take is $5,000 down, and the remainder to be paid at $3,000 per year."

It was all Evangeline could do to maintain enough decorum to see him to the door. When he was safely tucked into his car, Evangeline burst into her own private praise party. Once again God had managed the impossible for her. He provided property for 75 percent of the asking price and then provided the finances to close the deal. All of this, He did without Evangeline having a single penny in the bank.

Did God want the conference center to have the

recreation center property? Evangeline knew the answer. Yes. Absolutely.

By now, Evangeline had another dream simmering away in her mind. Conference center attendance continued to climb. Every season opened with the Christian Businessmen's Conference, followed by a week for Village Missions Retreat, and then one of the youth weeks. The other youth week was tucked away at the end of the summer, just before Labor Day weekend. The "new" chapel and dining hall, built just 10 years before, enabled the conference center to host many more guests for chapel services and meals than it could accommodate in guest housing. She never had enough room to house the people who wanted to stay. It was very clear to her that more guest rooms were needed.

So, she approached her friend and designer Gordon Nickell. Together, they made plans to build an eight-unit building near the new gymnasium. Their goal was to construct additional family housing as deluxe as possible on a very limited budget. The rooms would be spacious—eighteen feet from partition to partition. And, most exciting of all, each room would contain a bathroom with a shower! Never before had the conference center considered such luxury.

Once again, the purchase of materials would be the most difficult part of adding another building. The conference center did not charge its summer guests enough to cover its operations, let alone save toward additional building capital. Evangeline determined to contact her friend and lumber dealer, Mr. Miller. He was gracious enough to again respond with the needed lumber. By the summer of 1957, the eight units near the creek were open for guests. The new building was called the "Anchorage."

The new units were a success the moment they were opened. Demand again outstripped supply. With careful thought, they considered removing an old warehouse which was between the new unit and the main grounds. Without the warehouse, the new Anchorage could be continued, with an additional six units, all the way to the driveway. Again the plans were drawn.

Later that summer, Evangeline received some bad news from her brother Haldane. He reported reading of the death of Mr. George Miller in the Portland paper. Evangeline was saddened by the loss of her gruff, but faithful lumber friend. She wrote a long letter of sympathy to Mrs. Miller. "We, at the conference center, have been so very grateful for all his gifts of lumber. I have often heard much about his endeavors for the Lord. He was certainly a 'Prince among men.'"

At Christmas that year, Mrs. McNeill received a very strange Christmas card. It was signed, "Your dead friend, George Miller." He explained the coincidence— that in Portland, a man with the same name had died. But, the man was not he. "Your letter was certainly a surprise to my wife, but she has recovered nicely. Not many men have the good fortune of reading their own letters of condolences. But I assure you, I appreciated the many fine things you said about me. And, Mrs. McNeill, if you have any further need of lumber, you have only to let me know."

By summer of 1959, the six additional units of the Anchorage were finished. Needless to say, they were built with lumber donated by Mr. Miller, who was very much alive.

Evangeline came to the end of that summer season with a great sense of peace in her heart. Yes, this decade had been a difficult one. She experienced great loss. But, she had also known the pleasure and satisfaction of being in the very center of God's will. She witnessed His miraculous provision. She knew His guidance. An exciting new decade stretched out before her. She knew that He would continue to lead. He would continue to provide. She sensed a season of growth waiting for her and for her work. Yes, she looked forward to the new year.

13

Expansion

Evangeline had a great many plans for the 1960s. It would be a season of expansion. There was so much potential. So much to do.

The decade began with the removal of some of the outbuildings located on the Rec Center property. They were simply dangerous. In addition, a serious winter storm had destroyed most of the seawall that protected the village of Cannon Beach. Each property owner along the ocean was required to pay for the new seawall. The expense was a hardship for the conference center. But once again, God provided the funds. The wall was built of log pilings.

God provided more than funds for Evangeline. Her brother Walter, now the full-time director of Village Missions, was living in Dallas, Oregon. Having him so close was a source of constant comfort and help to her. Many times, when a plane was delayed or a speaker became suddenly ill, Walter's phone would ring in the early morning hours. Evangeline would explain her dilemma, and in no time at all, Walter was on his way to fill in for the missing speaker. He could be counted on for advice, to find volunteers, or to handle any unexpected emergency.

The strong ties in the Duff family enabled Evangeline to be a giver as well. Her brother, Haldane, established a thriving conference ministry of his own in the Seattle area known as Park of the Pines. Haldane's ministry benefited from using many of the musicians and speakers his sister discovered. Whatever resources they had, they shared.

Nearly all of Evangeline's nieces and nephews were able to spend summers working at the conference center. There, they found many treasures: new friends, new responsibilities, new skills, and a mother away from home. For most of the nieces and nephews, it became their first opportunity to try their hand at adult working relationships. It was also one of their first exposures to Christianity in action outside the narrow circle of their immediate family.

Evangeline had long been a friend of Edna Frisbee, the elderly widow of the man who originally owned the conference center property. Edna was the same age as Evangeline's mother, Mathilda Duff. The two old ladies had enjoyed one another's company. As Mrs. Frisbee grew older, Evangeline would often visit Edna, take her an occasional meal, or drive her to a doctor's appointment. Evangeline was concerned about Edna's health.

Edna Frisbee still owned land adjacent to the conference center. Often Evangeline spoke to Edna about the possibility of buying the remaining parcel. Edna would never consider such a sale. "Oh, Evangeline, there will be plenty of time to worry about that," she would say. If Edna died without selling, Evangeline worried that her heirs would not sell to the conference center.

Evangeline was genuinely grieved when Mrs. Frisbee suddenly passed away. Her death was unexpected. She was even more surprised when she was contacted by Mrs. Frisbee's attorney. It seemed that Edna Frisbee, a devout Christian Scientist, named Mrs. Evangeline McNeill, "her devoted friend," as heir to the land adjacent to the conference center. She left a large portion of her estate to the Christian Science Church. She had been unwilling to sell Evangeline the property because she always intended to give it to her.

What a remarkable provision. This last parcel along with an unused strip of conference land formed a large section where they could now build additional guest facilities.

Many of the original conference buildings were quickly aging and required constant upkeep. As they aged, they became less and less frequented by the families who came to the conference center. It was clear to Evangeline that new lodgings were needed. She asked Gordon Nickell to design plans for a building that would fit the unusual angles of the property. This he did. The new building would be a large flying wedge shape, completed in three sections. The first portion would be the wing facing the inner garden area of the conference grounds. It would have eight rooms on each floor, accessed by a hallway behind the rooms. Toward the garden, each room had its own lanai with sliding patio doors. The private bathroom and garden view made these rooms the most luxurious at the conference center.

As usual, Mrs. McNeill began her building project with not a penny set aside. The money, materials, and labor would come in as they were needed. They always had. She was confident that they would again.

The Columbus Day storm of 1962 badly damaged the tar paper roof of the Anchorage building. But it was not until the following January that a repair crew could gather at the conference center. While one crew repaired the roof, another poured the footings for the new lodge.

This building, like those before it, was built entirely by volunteer labor. When materials or workers were available, the project proceeded steadily. But whenever they ran short of supplies or men, the entire undertaking came to a halt. At times the lack of progress was discouraging. Each time things slowed, Evangeline prayed. God answered, and the first wing was in use by summer 1963. Evangeline was grateful for its rapid completion. She wrote in her conference newsletter dated October 1963,

"Did you know the lumber for the new building was a gift? The architectural plans... a gift? The beautiful patio doors on the lower level... a gift? The plumbing was met by interested friends who gave gifts of $100. The cement pouring was a gift. The electrical installation... a gift. The lighting fixtures... a gift, and Mr. Roland Casey, the contractor in charge, gave hours and hours of time and effort in dedication to the task, assisted by other gifted men."

It was a beautiful, motel-style building provided entirely by the loving gifts and donated hours of many conference center friends.

Evangeline paused for only a moment to enjoy the success of the building project. She made plans to complete the next portion of the three-stage project. After securing the lumber, she stored it at the end of the property near the creek. Then in the spring of 1964,

God Himself became more actively involved in her building plans.

On the Friday of Holy Week, March 27, 1964, Evangeline made plans to celebrate the birthday of her good friend and staff member Winnie Argenbright. After sending Winnie into Seaside to an evening church service, Evangeline decorated her home for the surprise party. By the time Winnie returned, the house was full of well wishers. They enjoyed a delicious cake, and there was much laughter. By 11 o'clock, everyone had gone. Evangeline retired.

Sometime later, Evangeline woke to pounding on her door. What could this be? she thought, reluctant to get up again. When at last she opened the door, she discovered Polly, a staff member. "Quickly, Mrs. McNeill, there is a tidal wave. There was an earthquake in Alaska, and we're just getting the water now. Hurry. The water is coming up."

Evangeline woke Winnie, and dressed in their night-clothes, the three women scurried up the ladder leaning against her carport . Safely perched on the roof, they watched with wonder as the water steadily rose. It was a beautifully clear night, with a full moon giving the eerie sensation of daylight. As the water rose, a duplex floated up the creek and settled in the field across from the conference grounds. It was followed by the bridge which used to cross the creek on the way into town. The bridge had not fared nearly so well as the house. It had broken into pieces with large logs floating by as they watched. The water continued to rise. They realized that they would need to escape via the south end of town to avoid becoming stranded.

Carefully they got down off the roof and headed by rowboat for higher ground. Evangeline spent a restless night at a friend's home.

The next morning Evangeline was not sure what, if anything, she would find remaining at the conference center. She was anxious to go back and account for the damage. Together, she and Winnie and Polly returned to the grounds.

To their surprise, there was very little damage to the buildings. Naturally, the first floor of the new building had water damage. The carpets would need to be pulled up and cleaned. But remarkably, the logs that had floated by the conference grounds had lodged themselves solidly against the bank of the property near the creek. They were massive logs, which protected the conference grounds from mountains of debris which floated up the creek and landed on adjacent property. In addition, the lumber which was stored near the creek, was prevented by the logs from floating back down the river when the water receded. In time, the lumber would dry.

The water, which carried with it large quantities of silt, had left the silt behind, filling in the very low ground on the creek end of the conference center. God himself protected the property, while at the same time bringing in more fill dirt than the conference center could afford to purchase on its own. Even in disaster, God managed the impossible.

The water damage, experienced all over Cannon Beach, changed the city's viewpoint on construction safety. All new buildings were required to be built above a new high water mark. This meant that the second phase of the new lodge, where the new registration area, lobby, snack bar, and book store would be located, had to be elevated two full steps above the first phase.

Those who built the second phase worried that the difference would be distracting to observers. Certainly people would wonder about this strange "misplanning" of elevation. They would never know that those two strange looking steps were the unavoidable result of an earthquake whose epicenter was over 1,500 miles away.

This second phase also housed a second floor meeting room which would seat about 200 people. It was Evangeline's dream to have another location to hold smaller gatherings during the off-season. The smaller room would have better lighting and be easier to heat in the winter. Its unusual shape lent itself perfectly to the placement of a small platform overlooking the south lawn area. The second floor had large windows and sliding glass doors which led to a wrap around porch. The meeting room was accessible to the second floor guest wings on both sides of the building.

When the time came to build the second phase, Evangeline assembled her reliable crew of volunteer help. The unusual angles in the new building plan demanded that every floor and ceiling joist be hand cut to the exact angles required by the plans. This was more than even her most committed volunteers were willing to try.

Evangeline called the building designer in Seattle. "Gordon do you think you and Emmet Peterson could come down and help us? Not a carpenter who comes to the conference will touch those beams. They're afraid to do it."

"Evangeline, do you mean the designer has to come down and erect all those beams in self-defense?" Gordon laughed.

"Well," she said, "it rather looks that way."

Of course Gordon and Emmet would drive down to Cannon Beach to help. They packed their cars with their tools and said good-by to their families. As she kissed her husband, Austa Nickell asked with a chuckle, "Is there anything you won't do for that red-headed widow?"

"Now, dear Austa," Gordon answered back, "how much help do you think she would get if she weren't such a charming and beautiful red-headed widow?"

At the conference grounds, Emmet and Gordon carefully cut and erected each beam, pair by pair until finally all the hips and valleys of the roof were in place.

"Well you did it!" Evangeline exclaimed happily when it was finished.

"Of course we did," Gordon replied. "Simple geometry—nothing more. And not only are all those beams in place, we did it without running out of timbers. We came out exactly right—we didn't cut any of the beams twice."

"Oh, well, you ordered them didn't you?" She asked.

"Yes, I did," he replied.

"Well, then you should have been right!" she concluded.

The second phase of the new building was completed by the next season. As usual, Evangeline found ways of saving money in order to do it. The carpet came at a bargain price from the platform of the Billy Graham crusade held in Portland. "Why it's as good as new!" she exclaimed. When the time came to put in light fixtures, she asked Gordon what he had in mind.

"Well," he replied, "I was thinking of 16-inch globes."

Evangeline headed to Portland to look for globes. Of course she prayed about her mission. But, she was not surprised to have the lighting man tell her that 16 inch globes were not in demand at all any more. "In fact, they are a burden for me to store. I can let you have them for less than I paid for them." She came home with fixtures that were almost free.

By 1967, the third and final stage of the guest building which became East and North Haven was complete. Conference attendance continued to climb. Her schedule of conferences expanded to include eight spring and four fall events. These off-season conferences were her biggest challenge. It was difficult to get staff to come work for a single isolated weekend. She found college students who brought friends and came to work at the beach. They worked very hard for the weekend, and were able to earn a little extra money. They also found some free time to enjoy the beach. Planning these off-season conferences required that she spend the winter in Oregon. So, while she continued to start Clubs and Council groups for the Christian Women's Club, she no longer did it from Stonecroft.

Life was changing for Evangeline in many ways. Heather had long since graduated from college, and after teaching school for some time, was now working in Washington D.C.. Helen Jean was nearly grown as well. Having adult daughters enabled Evangeline to focus all her energy on traveling, speaking, and of course, on the ministry of the conference center.

As the sixties drew to a close, Evangeline reflected on what the Lord had accomplished. The conference center ministry was thriving. She hosted such nationally known speakers as Dr. J. Vernon McGee, Dr. Allen Redpath, and Reverend John Hunter. These men, together with the modern accommodations and outstanding location of the conference center, had thrust the center into its largest decade of growth. Years ago, she and Archie planned to minister extensively to young people. But God seemed to have changed her course. Now, she ministered mainly to adults and families. It was no longer a camp. It was a resort. It looked as though God had moved her into a new kind of ministry without her even realizing it had happened.

14

Bits and Pieces

The ringing telephone interrupted Wanda's thoughts. "Ugh, why does that thing only ring when I am in the middle of something?" Backing out on her hands and knees, she unfolded herself off the bathroom floor, and carefully removed her rubber gloves. The floor was half washed. Oh well. The ringing continued.

"Hello Wanda, honey. This is Evangeline."

Her irritation turned to delight. Evangeline McNeill was a long time friend. Neil and Wanda Fisher were Village Missionaries working in Bridge, Oregon.

Evangeline explained that she was helping to start a Christian Woman's Club in Myrtle Point. Normally starting a club involved holding a luncheon where local women could gather to see some special program, a style show or demonstration, which was followed by a guest speaker. Evangeline was planning this latest luncheon.

"You know Wanda, when I was at your house the last time, you made the most delicious cinnamon twists. I wonder. Could I ask you to make enough of those for 100 women? They would dress up the plates so much."

Wanda was glad to make the rolls. She was active in Christian Women's Clubs, and believed in the ministry as a way to win women to Christ. Baking the twists would be no problem.

"And honey, do you think you could get some of the ladies from your church to volunteer to help set up, and clean up? Then, we will need some ladies to serve tables and some others to host the tables."

Wanda chuckled to herself. Baking rolls was nothing compared to finding volunteers. "Sure, Mrs. McNeill. How many women do you need?"

Once the details were explained, Wanda did not see or hear from Evangeline again until the day of the luncheon. That morning, at the appointed hour, Wanda met the other volunteers at the rented hall. Mrs. McNeill had not yet arrived. The tables were there. The kitchen was ready. But Wanda was surprised to find that no one had begun to cook the food.

Just then, Mrs. McNeill drove up in her big old green Oldsmobile. Moving at her usual clip, she jumped out of the driver's seat, called out her greeting to the ladies and proceeded to open the trunk. There, to Wanda's amazement, was the food which would feed 100 ladies. With remarkable efficiency, Evangeline instructed the ladies in setting up tables and decorating the hall.

While the ladies prepared the dining room, Evangeline went to the kitchen and prepared the food. Wanda had no idea who would be doing what. But she certainly had not expected Evangeline to cook for that many people. Soon, delicious smells came wafting from the kitchen.

The dining room was ready. The food was ready. Evangeline called the volunteers who would be serving the meal to the kitchen, and gave them last minute instructions. Then she disappeared into the restroom.

Wanda was again surprised to see Mrs. McNeill emerge beautifully dressed and madeup, with a lovely luncheon hat. She went to the doors and began to graciously greet her guests.

The program went completely as planned. The food was very good, and the guests were enjoying themselves. At last, the speaker was introduced. Who should get up to speak but Mrs. McNeill of Cannon Beach Christian Conference Center? Wanda was enjoying her secret. How surprised these ladies would be to know that the guest speaker was also the cook. Nothing about Mrs. McNeill's graciousness or composure gave any hint of the things she had done that morning. With a gentle opportunity to accept Jesus as Savior, the luncheon was closed. Mrs. McNeill unhurriedly chatted with women as they exited the hall.

Wanda and her crew had just cleared the tables, when Mrs. McNeill joined them in the kitchen. Her clothes were changed again. The luncheon hat left behind. She was soon up to her elbows in dirty dishes.

Even though the volunteers were very tired, Wanda noticed that not one of them left the rented hall that day before Mrs. McNeill. They helped her load the leftovers into her trunk, and warmly thanked her for all she had done.

As Wanda drove the five miles home, she was struck by what she witnessed. Never had she seen anyone work harder. Never had she seen a more gracious and humble effort to win women to Christ. Cook, Supervisor, Advertising, Clean up, and Speaker. Evangeline McNeill did all these things without notice. Without fanfare. Without thanks.

After a long and exhausting day, Evangeline slipped into a deep sleep. The phone had been ringing for quite some time before she could get her mind alert enough to respond. Her limbs felt sluggish and heavy. At last she answered.

The voice on the other end was full of alarm. "My friend has run away. I tried to talk to him but he just won't listen to me." The young male voice continued, "Please. Can you help me? He swallowed a full bottle of sleeping pills just before he left. I think he is headed for the beach. I would go after him. But I know he needs someone who can do more. Someone who can get through to him. I called his parents and they said to call you. What can you do?" The voice rose in panic.

"We will pray and we will look." Evangeline's voice was calm and reassuring. She was wide awake by now. This kind of call was not unusual. People around Cannon Beach knew that Evangeline McNeill was available at all hours of the day to help in any emergency. But what could she do for this young boy? How could she help when his friend could not? As she hung up, she gave him what assurance she could. Then she started to pray.

The phone rang again. It was the missing boy's mother. "We are on our way," she assured Evangeline. "But, it will take us nearly three hours. Please," she begged, "do what you can."

It was three a.m. Quickly Evangeline called her secretary. Lucille appeared at her door dressed and ready to help a few minutes later. Together they prayed and headed for the car. Where would they look? Driving along the beach was treacherous, even in the daylight. They agreed to start by checking downtown.

to say. But still,
e asked to join
t, she resigned
ady stayed past
e no longer had

Ann could not
nt. It seemed as
an living in her

peaceful. She
ct, she seemed
er death.
xpected to find.
e asked Emma
ted to tell her
ine McNeill.
something she
s a new term to
ned the phrase,
sed. The Sister
life. Now, this
life was a gift.
or by the blood
o do was accept

of my religious
st be mistaken.
sedatives had
no denying the
, tearful, timid,

As they turned onto mainstreet, their headlights caught a lone figure walking quickly through town.

Mrs. McNeill slowed the car and rolled down her window. The figure slowed as well. She asked the young man's name. Without hesitation he gave it. They found him! He was dazed but coherent. Evangeline explained who she was and asked him to get into the car. He complied.

Both ladies understood the importance of getting the boy to the hospital. Evangeline started for Seaside. As they passed the conference grounds, the boy became agitated. "Are you taking me to the hospital? I thought you said you were taking me to the conference grounds. I am getting out right now."

Evangeline swung the car around saying, "We are going to my house. How about something hot to eat?"

When he found the house warm and cozy, he began to relax. Lucille fixed him some hot chocolate, while Evangeline called his parents. They had not left yet.

As Evangeline was instructed, she called the doctor on duty at the Seaside Hospital. "You must not let him go to sleep under any circumstances," he urged her. "Call the police and have him brought right in."

After losing precious minutes contacting the police, she found them unwilling to help. "It is a matter for an ambulance," they told her. Evangeline was desperate. The boy had fallen asleep. The ambulance in Cannon Beach was out on another call. She and Lucille prayed again. They could not get him into the car by themselves. The phone rang. It was the ambulance crew. "We just finished our last call. We heard you needed some help. What can we do for you?"

Evangeline explained her situa
utes the crew was loading the uncon
ambulance. She and Lucille followee
Seaside. The emergency room crew
stomach was pumped. He was aliv

It was an exhausted Evangeline
back to the conference center. "You
Lucille said sleepily, "you need to a
being available to everyone on the C
ever anyone needs you. You can't
looking for runaways. You need y
keep this up forever."

"Lucille," Evangeline answer
would that young man be if we
tonight? I know you care. I appre
are right. Maybe I can't keep this s
But for now, I can. And, for as lc
ask me I will be available."

The woman who stepped fro
hardly what Sister Barbara Ann h
woman was beautifully dressed ii
the latest style. Her hair was a go
swept up into a coil behind her he
perfectly applied. Her jewelry, a l
conservative, exactly set off the

This lady evangelist was tho
dowdy or poor. She was not at al
Sisters in Pendleton, Oregon ex
knew what to expect. But they ha
communal speculation. None ad
evangelist" in person before. B
she was a glorious sight.

listen to what this unique woman had
she hoped somehow that she would I
them. When it was clear she would n
herself to leaving the floor. She had alre
her shift to meet the lady evangelist. Sh
an excuse to stay.

The next morning, Sister Barbara
believe the change she saw in her patie
though Emma Smith had a new wom
old frail body.

The new woman was happy and
certainly was no longer afraid. In fa
somehow to glow in anticipation of h
This was not at all what the Sister e
Her curiosity got the best of her and s
for an explanation. Emma was delig
nurse all about her visit with Evangel

The essence of Emma's joy was
called "Justification by Faith." This wa
Sister Barbara Ann. After Emma expla
Sister Barbara Ann was even more conf
spent years working to obtain eternal
old sick woman told her that eternal
Her's for the asking. Bought and paid
of Jesus Christ. All the dear nurse had t
the gift.

How could this be? How could all
training be wrong? Certainly Emma m
She has some confusion— perhaps th
affected her reasoning. But there was
change in Emma. She had been edgy

and frightened. Now she was full of laughter, smiles and peace. Emma Smith was relaxed, lucid. Perhaps there was something to what she said.

Mrs. McNeill returned several times to visit Emma. Each time, Sister Barbara Ann found an excuse to ask her about some point of her religious beliefs. Sister began attending a small Bible study at Opal's home. Evangeline realized that Sister Barbara Ann was genuinely hungry to know more about spiritual things.

On one particular visit, Mrs. McNeill was leaving Emma's room when Sister caught her. They went to their usual place in the consultation room. There the two women conversed undisturbed from 11 o'clock in the morning until nearly five in the evening.

"For it is by grace you have been saved, through faith—and this not from yourselves. It is the gift of God—not by works, so that no one can boast." (Ephesians 2:8,9 NIV) Evangeline didn't tell Sister Barbara Ann that she planned her visit to include the nurse as well as the patient.

This was the beginning of a long and difficult process for Sister Barbara Ann. Somehow she needed to resolve the difference between her religious teaching and the Bible. At first, she laughingly proclaimed, "If ever I am excommunicated, I will become a Presbyterian—like Mrs. McNeill."

But the laughter didn't last long. Her growing faith blossomed. She knew that she must leave the convent. This involved great risk— would she be released from her vows? She knew of rumors that other nuns wanting to leave had been committed to mental institutions. Her decision was not easy. She would leave—suddenly, without warning. With the help of her friend Opal and a local pastor, she left everything behind.

It was Opal's idea for Sister Barbara Ann to travel with Mrs. McNeill, who was obligated to a full schedule of speaking engagements. It was a way to remain safely out of sight. Opal heard that Sister Barbara had been declared insane. The rumors indicated that the Oregon State Patrol had been asked to bring her back to Pendleton. Traveling with Mrs. McNeill would keep her moving until her legal options were clear.

But Sister Barbara Ann, whose real name was Marjorie Collier, was appalled by the prospect. "I have no clothes. I have no hair. A woman in a crew cut cannot possibly go with you to ladies' luncheons."

"Oh, yes you can," Evangeline replied. "Try this on."

Obediently, Marge placed the close fitting flapper style hat on her head. The fit was perfect. The hat covered her entire bald head, except for the small curl that dangled from her forehead. It worked. No one would suspect that she had anything less that an elaborate hairdo under the hat.

"It is a hat I bought on my way through Chicago." Evangeline continued, sparkling in the fun of the disguise. "I don't know why I bought it. It really never looked good on me. And, after I took it back to my hotel, I decided that I needed to return it. But somehow, the Holy Spirit just wouldn't let me. I didn't understand until now—The Holy Spirit had me buy that hat for you!"

The two women went to luncheon after luncheon. A deep respect and affection grew between them. They were almost sad when they learned that a nursing position had been found for Marjorie. Their travels came to an end. But their friendship did not. Not a week went by that Marjorie did not write a loving and newsy letter to her friend. Evangeline came to look forward to the pink envelopes from Medford, Oregon.

Each envelope contained some new problem or question that Marjorie encountered in her effort to become a sincere disciple of Christ. This week she asked about the souls of innocent miscarried babies. The next letter requested instruction on witnessing to a new patient in her hospital. With great patience, Evangeline tried to help Marge along. She sent tapes, or a pertinent scripture. Every time Evangeline heard from Marjorie, her heart was glad that she had answered a friend's request to visit a lady in a Pendleton hospital.

The bedroom door opened gently. Soft yellow light tumbled into the room from the hall. A small figure walked quietly toward her bed, and knelt beside it. Marty rolled and stretched in an effort to wake up. They had traveled all day and she was so tired. What could Evangeline possibly want from her now?

"You know, Marty, I love you so much," Evangeline said quietly. Then, she stroked her hair and stood to leave. The door was shut as quietly as it had opened.

Marty's eyes filled with tears. Evangeline's love was something she never quite understood. It felt so good. No one in Marty's life had ever loved her in quite the same way. No matter what she looked like, what mischief she was in, Evangeline loved her. It was as simple as that.

Marty let her weary mind drift back over the years to her first visit to the conference center. She had just made a personal commitment to Christ. Her family rarely attended church and she had little opportunity to grow in her newfound faith. So, Marty's best friend invited her to join the family for part of a week at the Cannon Beach Conference Center. Marty remembered that week as one of the most wonderful in her life. The speaker spent the entire time talking about Jesus. This was so new and so special to Marty that she determined she would come again to the next year's youth camp. And she did— every year until she was at last old enough to join the summer staff waiting tables.

Even working at the conference center happened in a roundabout way for Marty. Heather McNeill, Marty's friend, helped her get a summer job cleaning rooms at the motel near the conference center. But after she started work, Marty discovered that the motel owner was unwilling to let Marty attend church on Sunday. Marty was bitterly disappointed. When Heather let her mother know, Evangeline responded by offering Marty a job waiting tables at the conference center. She was delighted to accept.

It turned out to be a wild summer. The 10 or 12 girls who lived above the administration office spent the summer dreaming about the boys who were also on staff. They whispered and giggled, sang together and shared clothes. Marty was struck by the fact that the young people who worked at the conference center were by no means perfect people. Some were quite mature in their Christian faith. Others, like herself, were not.

Marty was a very attractive young woman. Before

coming to the conference center, she had done some modeling in southern Oregon. In the last style show, her hairdresser had put a red streak in her hair. The other kids saw it as sign of Marty's worldliness. While they might make unkind comments toward her, Mrs. McNeill never did. Mrs. McNeill always made her feel like she was loved. Like she belonged.

It was during this first summer that something special happened in Marty's life. She worked very hard. And, as part of the summer activity, the "wait staff" was invited to join in the teaching sessions for the youth camp that occupied the last week of the summer. Marty was taken by the speaker. He spoke frequently about the need to fully dedicate your life to Jesus Christ. On the last night, he gave the youth an opportunity to come forward in dedication. Marty wanted to respond. But, she had endured so much teasing, she was reluctant to give the staff something more to tease her about. Then, she felt a tap on the shoulder. It was the boy who sat behind her. "Why don't you go forward?" he said. It was all the encouragement she needed.

She went home a changed young woman. It was the first time she ever recalled wanting to give every part of herself to Jesus. She went home determined to make a difference in her school. She would witness. She would let her friends know that she was a Christian.

Marty spent every summer at Cannon Beach growing deep roots in her relationship to the Lord.

When Marty announced that she had entered her first beauty pageant, Mrs. McNeill was supportive, despite her own misgivings. Marty smiled to herself when she remembered Heather telling her what her mother said. "How could anyone parade around in a bathing suit in front of an audience?" But, Evangeline McNeill softened when she realized the new opportunities that Marty would have to share her faith.

Alone, Marty reflected in the dark. Her smile turned into a quiet giggle. Yes, Mrs. McNeill had certainly figured out how to help Marty share her faith.

Here she was, Miss Oregon 1962, driving around in Mrs. McNeill's big old oldsmobile. Some life of glamour. Every night a different town— a different church— a different home to stay in. Marty groaned— a different bed. Evangeline planned their itinerary weeks before they left Cannon Beach. Marty knew she was nothing more than bait. Evangeline was one of the world's great fishermen. They had been together four long weeks. Often, another person joined them. Another bait. An opera singer. A famous pianist. Miss Oregon.

At first, Marty begged not to put on her big formal hooped dress for each evening's meetings. "But dear," Evangeline countered, "many of these people have never seen anyone look as beautiful as you do all dressed up in your formal dress. Do it for them."

Marty did it. Night after night, she would dress in her beautiful dress and give her testimony. Evangeline followed with a little salvation message of her own.

They were nearing the end of the road trip. Marty was dead tired. She looked forward to spending two nights in the same bed. Well, she thought dreamily as she rolled over and drifted off to sleep, it had certainly been an experience. She knew how to share her faith.

She was more comfortable in front of an audience. And most importantly, some of Evangeline's zeal toward unbelievers had rubbed off on Marty. "Yes," Marty said to the darkness, "I love you too, Evangeline."

15

A Change for Nick

ick entered the Umatilla County Courthouse this morning with a sense of hope mixed with great fear. It was clear, even to his 12-year-old mind, that he was in big trouble. Caught and charged with vandalism and burglary, he realized how serious this court hearing would be. He wasn't really sure his dad would attend.

Yet, here he was. Nick had only seen his father in a suit once before. That had been at the funeral. Everyone wore a suit to a funeral. But here was Nick's father, dressed in his brown suit. Certainly this was a big day.

Nick hoped that his father's presence marked the beginning of something new in their family— a new commitment— a new presence. Surely the judge would slap Nick's hands and turn him over to the custody of his newly committed father. Perhaps now, in spite of so much pain, dad would really try to build a family.

The judge was finished, and the sentence pronounced. Nick turned to his father. The forgiveness he hoped to see in his father's eyes was missing. Instead his face was tense with anger, and the words spilled out of his mouth. "You are not my son. You never were my son. You're nothing. If you ever get out of there, don't you ever come back. You'll never live in my house again."

Though his hope was dashed, Nick was not surprised. This was the father he knew best. Nick saw the truth in his father's words. There was no hope. He had been cast adrift and now he was completely alone.

Alone, he watched the door of his green steel cage slam shut. Listening to the retreating footsteps of the guard, Nick found himself with a single steel bed, a steel sink, and toilet and a cascade of memories. Nick had plenty of time to think.

His mind drifted back over the years. He wondered why this solitude was so painful. So strong. For as long as he could remember, Nick and his brothers and sisters had been on their own. How many times had his mother left home with some new man? How many times had alcohol taken his father away from the family? How many nights, holidays, and weekends had the children been left alone. Without food. Without clothing. Without love. Still, something inside of Nick had hoped today would turn out differently.

Looking out of the small window in his cell, he pondered the twinkling lights which marked the homes in the valley below. As the twilight deepened, the lights grew brighter. Each light a home, a face, a family.

Then as the stars began to appear, Nick was drawn to the enormity of the universe. If there was a God, how immense and diverse was His creation.

Again a memory returned to him. It was the funeral of his brother. Nick seethed with anger at God that day. How could a good God allow such a tragic death? Nick remembered wondering how he could ever live without Tom. Tom had been the only goodness in their family. Before he died, Tom told Nick about becoming a Christian. Nick didn't understand what Tom meant, but he could clearly see the difference it made in Tom's life. Some God, Nick had concluded. He lets His own people die.

But Nick also remembered having a strange — almost comforting experience at the funeral. Sitting in the service, Nick had heard a voice.

"It's all right Nick. It's OK. He's with me."

The voice seemed so real to Nick, that he remembered looking around to find the one who had spoken.

Now, as the twilight deepened into blackness, Nick wondered again about the voice. If he really had heard it, maybe there truly was a God. Nick knew something about God and sin. As a child, he occasionally attended Sunday School. Certainly, he reasoned, the long list of charges the police officer read in court today constituted sin. So, slowly, one by one as the nighttime hours passed, Nick told God everything he had done. Then as dawn began to break, a broken young boy said, "God, if you could forgive me, I need it. And if you could do anything with this life, I give it to you. I'll do anything you ask. And God, if you could love me, I really need that too."

As the sun came up that morning, Nick found himself sitting in the very lap of God, experiencing the wonderful electric blanket hug that God can give a hungry soul.

It was a changed boy who left the courthouse the next day bound for the MacLaren Reform School. Though he was handcuffed, his heart was finally free.

Reform school in the early 1960s was a prison-like experience for Nick. One day, he was called to the Warden's office, where he was offered the opportunity to be released to a foster home. Total control and regular humiliation made him more than willing to consider such a move. Even though in those days, the foster home movement was so new that no one knew quite what to expect. There were more than 100 boy's names on the list waiting for placement. Nick's name was on the bottom. However one day, for some unexplainable reason, Nick found his name had moved to the top of the list.

Lee Huffsmith, who ran a Portland foster home with Youth for Christ, became Nick's first foster mother. It was in her home that Nick first sensed how real Christianity worked in the family environment.

Through Lee, Nick met Evangeline McNeill. On a beautiful spring day, Lee and Nick headed for the Oregon Coast in a new '64 Chevy station wagon. As they turned onto the conference grounds, Nick was taken immediately by its pristine beauty. He had never lived where beauty was a thing to work for just for the sake of enjoying it. Here, all around him were flowers and gardens and grass—just for the beauty of it all.

Then from across the grounds, he saw Mrs. McNeill. Her red hair was carefully coiled up on top of her head. She moved quickly and with purpose to her step. In a neatly pressed blouse and skirt, she waved across the grounds. Her smile was broad and genuine. Nick knew that he and Lee were unexpected guests today, yet he was surprised by the gracious and genuine warmth of Evangeline's greeting.

At this point, 13-year-old Nick was tentative. What

little self worth he possessed had been driven from him by institutional living. Yet here was a woman who seemed so genuinely glad to meet him, so full of effervescence. His gratitude for her graciousness would soon grow into deep respect and great love.

The conversation that day covered the possibility of the four foster boys from the Huffsmith home being employed for the summer as conference kitchen help. In spite of their delinquent background, Evangeline seemed delighted to have the boys join the staff.

One month later, summer found all four boys at the coast working long hard days as part of the dishwasher crew. The kitchen was hot, the equipment less than optimal and the boys found themselves constantly wet, and greasy. Their wrinkled fingers soon resembled prunes.

Because of their background, Evangeline kept a special eye on these boys. She was always checking to see that their needs were met. After a short time, she began to ask Nick to accompany her on her evening lockup rounds. In the dark, they shared bits and pieces of their past. Soon, Evangeline knew all about the lonely childhood that brought Nick to the Huffsmith home.

Nick was amazed by Evangeline. She seemed to oversee every detail of conference life. Her hands were part of every task. No matter how small or dirty, Nick found Evangeline involved in every job. Soon she was asking the boys to help in other areas of conference ministry.

On one particular evening Evangeline arrived in the kitchen in her evening formal. Nick knew that she was scheduled to play a concert harp solo for the evening service. He expected her to come in and check on their progress with the evening cleanup. Instead, Evangeline opened the refrigerator and removed an entire bag of clean carrots. With knife in hand, chopping furiously, she said, "Dear, can you give me a hand with these carrots?"

Together they chopped. Then, as suddenly as she arrived, she dried her hands and left for the chapel. Nick watched her hurry across the grounds to perform for the chapel guests. From her meticulous appearance, the guests would have no idea she came from working in the kitchen. Within minutes, she was back furiously chopping carrots again. Nick soon discovered that Evangeline's willingness to help in the kitchen, extended to every job on the grounds. Whatever she asked the boys to do, she was there alongside of them.

As the summer progressed, the special friendship between Evangeline and Nick grew. Nick began to accompany her on her weekly trips to Portland. Though the conference center had grown considerably, Evangeline still took care of buying groceries herself. Every week she took the little green truck, outfitted with stock racks, to Portland. On these trips they often picked up plywood, Formica, moldings, or any other building supply that was needed for the conference operation. Even young Nick found the trips exhausting.

But he still looked forward to the time alone with Evangeline. They headed up the highway together week after week. They would sing some, and talk a great deal. Nick would ask questions about the Lord, about Christianity and his new faith, and especially about things he had observed at the center. Lovingly and patiently, Evangeline began to build for Nick an understanding of the depth and scope of his new faith in Christ.

On one particular summer day Evangeline announced as they began their weekly trip that she needed 13 watermelons. Without hesitation she simply stopped and prayed aloud for her watermelons. Nick groaned to himself "Oh come on— NOBODY prays for watermelons."

The day progressed as usual. They purchased formica, curtain hardware, and bathroom fixtures. Then they proceeded to pick up the week's groceries. With their purchases carefully stuffed into the truck, they started to get into the truck cab. Their money was completely gone and still they had no watermelons. Nick didn't mention Evangeline's unanswered prayer, but he was sure they would head home without them. Just then Jimmy, the market owner came toward the truck.

"Mrs. McNeill," he said. "Would you have any use for watermelon? I have 13 out back that you can have if you can use 'em."

Nick went home that day with a new understanding of everyday faith.

Nick loved to attend the evening services. He would hurry through the dishes and arrive in time to hear the speaker. Like a sponge, Nick soaked up the rich teaching of great Bible teachers from all over the country. But his favorite event occurred after the service, when the regular guests left.

Frequently, Evangeline invited the speaker to her home for tea. Always she included Nick. Though he never understood why she invited a 13 year old to these adult gatherings, he relished every opportunity to listen to the personal side of the wonderful speakers who came to the conference.

It was in this way that Nick came to own his first Study Bible. The speaker, Dr. John Moore, was full of questions for Nick. "Of all the things you could get in your life, what would you want most?"

Nick answered, "I really don't have a decent Bible, and I'm a new Christian. I'd love to own a Scofield Bible."

Not long afterwards Dr. Moore's own Scofield Study Bible was sent to Nick. The inside cover was inscribed "To John M. Moore, Glasgow, Scotland." It was filled with his personal sermon and study notes. Nick began to devour the margin notes and carefully followed the studies. He came to realize his own deep respect and admiration for those in ministry.

Though Nick was moved from foster home to foster home, every summer he would end up back at Cannon Beach. Quitting his part-time winter job, he would head for a much less profitable job at the coast. As the summers progressed, Nick found himself leading the singing and playing trumpet solos for the conference guests. His special relationship with Evangeline continued to grow. He developed friendships that included other members of the staff. David Duff, a nephew of Evangeline and son of Village Missions director Walter Duff, became an especially close friend.

Each fall he returned to school until, at age 15 1/ 2, the state of Oregon discontinued his supervision and financial support. Determined to finish school, he returned to the Huffsmith home and rented a room.

Between pumping gas, and repairing and delivering copy machines, he was able to make ends meet. As graduation grew near, he faced the reality that college, for him, was out of the question. His only reasonable choice appeared to be career Military training. He began testing for enrollment in flight school.

Evangeline, however, had other plans for Nick. She told him with certainty that he should be preparing himself for full-time ministry. As she spoke, Nick recognized the truth of her words. But, to him the situation seemed hopeless. With no money, and no place to stay, Bible School seemed an unattainable goal.

Late in the summer after his high school graduation, Nick was back at the conference center. He was helping in the evening chapel service as usual. After he led the worship and the special music had begun, Evangeline took him aside and asked him to go over to the kitchen and check on dessert preparation. The request was so unusual that Nick hesitated slightly. But he went, and returned to the service to take the offering. It was then that three different men asked to meet Nick after the service and Nick discovered what Evangeline had done for him. "I believe," she had said to the congregation while Nick was away, "God wants that young man in ministry. He needs to attend Bible School this fall, and I believe that some family here could help by providing a place for him to stay."

Less than two weeks later, Nick, a tall robust man with sensitive deep brown eyes, was attending Bible School in Eugene, Oregon. Four years later, Nick and his bride were headed to their first pastoral position with Village Missions in Hawk Springs, Wyoming.

16

Ecola Hall

𝕴n 1971, at 67 years of age, Evangeline McNeill was in no mood for slowing down. During the last decade, the conference center at Cannon Beach had undergone incredible growth. In 10 years, Evangeline had led the construction of three major building projects. The new buildings were consistently filled. Attendance at summer conferences soared.

For the secular world, it was a decade of unrest. Besides the war in Vietnam, there was violence at home, on college campuses, and on city streets.

Evangeline felt that some cultural changes had also occurred inside the church. The decade of the 60s found liberalism firmly entrenched in many mainline churches. Evangelical churches, while maintaining their connection to the truth, fell into a mode of complacency. Church format varied little from church to church. While they had the truth, evangelical churches did little to respond to the culture war around them. Evangeline was keenly aware of her culture. She knew that the young people of the United States were increasingly dissatisfied with the answers being given them by the older generation. The demonstrations and violence were only a symptom of their dissatisfaction.

Evangeline's long-standing love and concern for young people came out again as this new generation turned its back on every tie to the traditions held sacred by their parents. She was forever speaking to the young people who wandered accidently onto the conference grounds as they looked for lodging. Many wore the trappings of their culture. It was the beatnik generation. They were long haired, unclean, and spoke a language all their own. But Evangeline was not shaken. She would take any opportunity to share with them about her Savior. Often she would stop to pray with some unsuspecting passerby. If he had no need that she could meet, she would be on her way. The stranger stood behind, shaking his head in wonder.

Evangeline was willing to try any method to reach the young people who wandered up and down the Pacific Coast in droves. So, when a young Portland couple came to her with a plan, she was excited to listen.

The old "Cannon Beach Recreation Center" building still stood on the beachfront property she had purchased in 1957. The conference center used the upper floor for staff housing, but the lower floor remained vacant. It included two store fronts accessible to the street. The plan was to turn one of these store fronts into a coffee house ministry. Here, the couple would try to reach young people with the gospel.

Evangeline knew that the rec center building would be demolished soon. She had plans to construct a new building on the sight as soon as plans and materials could be arranged. But until then, she reasoned, the property might have some eternal function. So, with her blessing one of the storefronts was cleaned, decorated, and opened to welcome young people.

David Duff, Evangeline's nephew and Walter Duff's youngest son, was also concerned about the aimless lives of the young people around him. He grew up in a Christian home, where Christian values were clearly demonstrated in his everyday life. His memories revolved around times spent at the conference center. It was there he made his first commitment to Christ. And there, seven years later, he first felt the call to Christian work.

From early adolescence through his first three years of college, summers found David Duff working in various capacities at the conference center. He worked in every building. He held nearly every job. The conference center was his home away from home. He considered aunt Evangeline his "summer mom."

In spite of the surety of his calling, David was confused about its details. After some consideration, he decided to attend Capernwray Hall, in Lancashire, Northern England. Located in an old English country home, the school had about 200 students living in dormitories on the school grounds. Teachers were guest lecturers, who came for one or two weeks of teaching.

Here, David became grounded in the systematic study and application of the Bible. It was a life-changing experience for him. Even though he had been exposed, as a child, to some of the most prominent Christian speakers of his day, he had not understood the Bible in a personal, methodical way.

While at school in England, he had the opportunity to spend his three-week Christmas break in London. He stayed in a flat belonging to medical students who had gone home for the holiday. In London, David was distressed by the faces of the young people he met in the streets. They seemed downcast, without hope. The English youth spent much of their time in the pubs. There were few jobs, and what little they earned went no further than an after work drink. Their hopelessness haunted David.

He spent time praying about what the Lord seemed to be saying through this experience. The thought occurred to him. Why not have a school like Capernwray in the United States? For that matter, why not have a whole string of them? Through the rest of the school term, the Lord continued to impress David with this need.

David returned to the United States and waited for just the right moment to share his idea. By midsummer, David had spoken about it with his parents, his aunt, Helen Baugh and her son Gordon. In the United States, the Jesus movement was bringing great tidal waves of young people to Christ. But few of these new believers had any means of becoming grounded in their faith. David's family saw how his idea could meet this need. With their enthusiastic support and encouragement, David invited a board to gather and consider the possibility of starting a short-term, non-accredited Bible school on the campus of Cannon Beach Christian Conference Center.

At the board meeting, David emphasized how many of the needed arrangements were already in place. The conference center facilities were completely unused during the winter months. They could easily house both the school and the students. Through the conference center, contacts for visiting instructors could be easily made. Between Village Missions, Christian Women's Councils and Clubs, and the conference center, there was a large audience for publicity.

Evangeline McNeill was delighted to work on the board of the new school. She and Archie had always dreamed that some kind of Christian school would occupy the conference grounds. Though she had no experience with this kind of school, she trusted David. Her instinct told her that now more than ever, the young people of this generation needed all the training they could get to successfully live the Christian life. Here was another answer to her growing concern for the strange young people she met on the streets and beaches of Cannon Beach.

She gave David her full support in readying the conference center to be used as a school. Most of buildings had not been winterized, so they began installing heating systems and insulation. The upstairs of the dining hall was unsuitable for use by students. It consisted of family-style rooms with double beds and no study areas. So the double beds were removed and bunks installed. New circuits were added to provide electricity to each room. Carpets were laid, rooms painted, and furniture placed. In the administration building, the boys dorm was renovated to provide additional student housing.

While they hammered and painted, the nearby Gearhart Hotel was closing. All of its furniture and fixtures were for sale. Evangeline and David made many trips to the hotel to purchase the remaining furniture. The lady in charge of the sale liked David. For Evangeline, her prices were stiff. But for David, invariably, her prices went down. Together, David and Evangeline obtained old carpets, old oak dressers, matching headboards and mirrors, restaurant chairs, and even an old ice machine.

As the school facilities were readied, David traveled to advertise its opening. His cousin, Gordon Baugh, enthusiastically agreed to help by contacting and scheduling the school's speakers. David contacted another cousin, Heather McNeill, who was working in the Washington D.C. area, and asked her to be the school's full-time secretary. She agreed, and moved back to Cannon Beach. Evangeline hired a cook, and found someone to supervise the food service for the winter months. Then she made arrangements for a winter maintenance man.

Gordon agreed to stay on as dean of the new school. His academic background included an extensive list of degrees from prestigious schools. Gordon would supervise finances, curriculum, speaker arrangements, student admissions, and discipline.

That first year, David and Evangeline determined tuition while leaning over a counter in the conference administration building. If tuition were too high, they would have no students. More than anything, they wanted the school to succeed. So they agreed that the first year's tuition would be $660 for three, eight week terms. This included room and board. It was a bargain they would never repeat.

David Duff would act as director of the school. Because he was talented and comfortable speaking in front of people, he chose responsibility for publicity, promotion, and student outreach teams. David would be in charge of the daily program and serve as the student chaplain.

Remarkably, the school was ready to open 12 months later. Applications began to arrive. This was, to all of them, another indication of the Lord's leading. In every turn, He seemed to be moving ahead of them.

They discovered another unexpected benefit from locating the school on the conference center campus. Evangeline had long wished for the grounds to be used during the winter, but many factors had prevented her dream from coming true. She regularly scheduled three weekend couples conferences every fall and spring. But it was nearly impossible for her to find enough staff to clean, cook and serve so many guests at this time of the year.

In the winter, many of her buildings were locked up and winterized. The water was off. The oil was drained. It was impossible to close the buildings, reopen them for a weekend conference or two, and then close them up again. Mrs. McNeill traveled for Christian Women's Councils and Clubs during the winter season to make financial ends meet over the nonproductive winter months. However, she found it difficult to keep her travel and speaking commitments and at the same time supervise a retreat schedule for the conference center.

The Bible School's presence on campus changed all that. Now, there were people on campus who could supervise meals, facilities and maintenance. She found herself with many students who needed financial help to pay for Bible school. They were willing workers who could clean rooms, serve meals, and help with facilities while attending school. The result was that with the Bible School in session, the conference center could provide retreat facilities for private groups of all sizes and denominations through the entire winter season. Mrs. McNeill chose to stay at Cannon Beach during the winter to help supervise what had become a year-round operation. Evangeline was delighted with the unexpected and wonderful side effect of having a school on the conference grounds.

17

Passing the Torch

As the decade of the 70s dawned, Evangeline wasted little time reflecting on past successes. She had one driving desire, and that was to plan and construct a building on the Rec Center property. Would it be a dining hall? Another meeting area? After much consideration and consultation with the city of Cannon Beach, they decided to build another guest building.

They dreamed of a building which included a large second-floor meeting room overlooking the ocean. The building would have a smaller dining hall and kitchen located directly below. It would house 20 guest rooms, 12 facing west toward the ocean and eight overlooking the north beach and the rocks of Ecola State Park. It was planned as an "adults only" building. For even though it was only one block from the registration desk, its location forced guests to cross two busy intersections. The building plans took several years to complete.

Before the new project could be constructed, the existing Rec Center building would have to be removed. Of course Evangeline didn't destroy the old building until every scrap of usable material was salvaged. Every window, every door, every plumbing fixture, all the extra wood, every little item was carefully removed and stored. Then the demolition began. A cable was tied around the center of the building and tightened until it actually cut the building in half. The building fell in on itself.

Her next step was to build a mammoth seawall. The western border of the Rec Center property was directly against the winter high water line. Raging winter storms and high tides characteristic of the Oregon Coast would be dangerous for the new building.

She knew nothing about such a task. While Gordon Nickell could draw the plans, she knew that safely building a giant seawall was more than she could expect from volunteers. This would take an expert. Evangeline did not know anyone with this kind of expertise, and she could not afford to purchase it. She began, as usual, to pray.

As Evangeline prayed, Warren Goss and his family were carefully planning their summer vacation. They were making a cross country auto trip from their home in Pittsburgh, Pennsylvania. They would start out by visiting their friend Helen Baugh at Stonecroft, in Kansas City, Missouri. Then, bit by bit, they would work their way across the United States.

By summer, the Goss family was delighted to leave the hot, sultry East Coast weather behind. While visiting Helen, they found Missouri was plagued by tornadoes. So, they headed for southern California. There, to their discouragement, they were forced to pay a tow truck to remove their family car from sandy Pismo Beach. This was not the vacation they dreamed about!

The Goss family decided to visit Yosemite National Park. There they ran straight into a forest fire. After much adversity, and no small amount of consternation, the Goss family unexpectedly arrived at the Cannon Beach Christian Conference Center. The cool coastal weather was a delightful change for them. They were thrilled with the speaker for the week. It looked, at last, like things were finally breaking their way.

That is, until Mrs. Evangeline McNeill stood up to introduce the evening speaker in a chapel service. Almost casually, she mentioned that she had been praying for the Lord to bring a man to Cannon Beach who knew how to build a seawall. That was the last thing Warren Goss wanted to hear—but her request was the last thing he really heard that evening.

Warren Goss owned a construction company that specialized in river walls. When he was introduced to Mrs. McNeill, her first question was, "Could you build us a seawall?"

"I never have. But I could if I wanted to," he replied. "But, I won't."

He couldn't resist Evangeline McNeill for long. Her enthusiasm was catching and her faith was inspiring. He agreed to speak to the designer about the plans. Evangeline called Gordon.

But Gordon Nickell had left Seattle to attend a wedding in California. Numerous calls missed him along the way. Warren Goss was leaving soon. If Evangeline couldn't contact Gordon, the seawall would not be built. Helen Baugh had come to the coast to visit her sister. They agreed that it was time to pray. And pray they did.

That evening, when the dinner bell rang, who

should enter the dining room but designer Gordon Nickell? Helen greeted him warmly. "Imagine seeing you here. Where have you been? We've called three states to locate you."

"Well now, have you?" Gordon chuckled. "What do you two need me for?"

"There is a man here from Pittsburgh who can build our wall. He wants desperately to talk to you. We wanted you to come down and speak with him."

"So, that explains it. Today we were heading north from California. When we came to the 'Y' in the road where we could choose to come up the coast highway or head up the freeway to Seattle, I just felt strongly that we should come by Cannon Beach. If you two prayed, it's no wonder that I am here."

Warren asked Gordon numerous technical questions as they visited after dinner. Their meeting was completed in less than an hour. Gordon and his wife Austa headed home to Seattle. Warren Goss made the decision to build his first seawall.

After studying the plans, he made a materials list and went to Portland to order the steel reinforcing rods. He rented a backhoe to do the trenching. He flew part of his crew out to Oregon from Pennsylvania. He recruited willing volunteers from the conference center. Together, right on the sight, they built and oiled the forms for the concrete . Then they poured the footings. When at last it was time to pour the seawall, the concrete started to flow at 8 a.m. The crew finished the continuous pour at 3 p.m.

The seawall was no small miracle. Warren and his wife both knew it. "You know honey," he said, the night the last of the forms were removed, "back home a project this size would have taken two months to complete. Here we finished in exactly six days. Only God could have done this."

"I know," she replied. "I have been thinking the same thing myself— how God used all those awful circumstances to bring us here. How we resisted the idea of building a seawall. You know, Warren, in all our wanderings, I have never felt so unquestionably used by God."

"Me too," he replied. "It's so powerful, it's almost scary."

Later that summer, Evangeline noticed a young man sitting alone at the Sunday service of the local Presbyterian church. He looks lonely, she thought, and invited him to join her for dinner at the conference center. "There are lots of young people there," she said. "You will enjoy yourself."

Steve did join her for dinner. Evangeline probed gently, wondering what brought this young man to Cannon Beach from his home in California. She discovered that he was on his way to Alaska. He planned to drive north until he ran out of funds. Then he would find a temporary job, and work until he could move on.

When Steve arrived at Cannon Beach, he found a construction project and asked the foreman if he could work for half the going wage. Steve was hired on the spot. As Evangeline listened to his story, she sensed his need for spiritual help.

Later that summer, she was glad to notice Steve attending one or two of the conference sessions. But, near the first of August, he came to say good-by. His job was through, and he would be moving on.

Evangeline was concerned. "Steve, perhaps you would consider staying on here. We are starting a new building project this fall. We could use an experienced carpenter." To her relief, he accepted.

What Evangeline did not know was that Steve was a heavy drinker. His drinking had caused him to be in a serious car accident earlier in the summer. As he lay in pain in the hospital, though not seriously injured, God began to speak to him. Steve was delighted to have a reason to stay near the conference center. He would gladly help with the new building.

The seawall was only the beginning of God's provision for what would become the Beachfront building. Evangeline planned to start construction during a "work week" in the fall of 1972. It was time to procure lumber. Her old friend George Miller had retired from the lumber business. His son, Bud Miller, now ran the mill. Evangeline went to see him. After she showed him her materials list, he was polite, but not definite as to what he would do. He asked for a copy of the list, and sent her on her way.

Several days later Evangeline noticed a letter from Bud Miller in her mail. Quickly she scanned it. "I would be glad to sell half of your lumber to you at wholesale prices." Evangeline paused, disappointed. She continued reading. "The remainder I would like to give you as our personal gift to the conference center." Yes, God continued to provide.

A builder from Spokane came to the beach to get the new beachfront building underway. During the first week, his skill, his power nailer and power equipment gave the building a good start. But he had to return to Spokane, so Steve continued building to the best of his ability. It became clear to Evangeline that Steve needed more experienced help. She prayed. Then, she received a phone call from a carpenter who was out of work. "Could you use some help?" he asked. Mike McIntyre went to work on the project.

This new guest unit was the largest, most complicated one the conference center had yet constructed. Mike longed to ask someone with more experience about the intricacies of the plans. But there was no one on campus to give construction advice.

Ecola Hall, a short-term nonaccredited Bible School, was just beginning its first year on the conference center campus. For many people—people of all ages and backgrounds— a small, less academic approach to Bible education was just what they wanted. One of these, a woman from Canada, wrote to the school: "I have always wanted a Bible school education. I would like very much to go to Ecola Hall. Do you take older people? Incidentally, my husband, who is a contractor, and I frequently leave Canada for a winter holiday. Would you have any use for his ability?"

Needless to say, they had plenty of use for a contractor.

As the work progressed, Evangeline delighted in God's anticipation of their every need. Though she was nearing 70 years old, she continued to oversee every detail of the construction. Her next concern was concrete. She became aware of a new technology that used light concrete to dampen sound traveling from floor to floor. Evangeline contacted local companies to obtain the correct materials. No one handled it. If the concrete were brought in from Portland, would the cost be astronomical? Just as she pondered the question, she remembered a nearby Tolovana family who attended summer conferences. It seemed to her that their business had something to do with light rock. She called them.

Mr. Schultz answered the phone himself. "Of course I understand, Mrs. McNeill. I know exactly what you need. Why don't I come to see you when I am up in Cannon Beach this weekend?"

When they were at last on the construction site, Mr. Schultz carefully examined the building. "Mrs. McNeill," he concluded, "it is the only way to go, but it is very costly. It will definitely do the job of quieting the building."

Evangeline was disappointed. "Well, if it's costly, we'll just have to forget it. We can't handle any added expense."

"Oh no, Mrs. McNeill," he said, "it's going to be a gift from us to the conference center."

In January of 1973, one of the outreach teams from Ecola Hall presented music in the Grays Harbor area of the Washington Coast. They spoke about all the happenings at the Cannon Beach Christian Conference Center. After hearing about the new building project, a subcontractor asked, "Is there a possibility that you would need any concrete work there? I am out of work most of January. If you need help in my line, I would be glad to come now."

God provided the concrete. God provided the concrete finisher.

Steve, the transient carpenter's helper, continued to work on the Beachfront building. He showed initiative and commitment. He was also fascinated by the presence of the Bible School on the grounds. Again, he came to Mrs. McNeill. "You know, Mrs. McNeill, I am building over there on the beach. But, my heart is over here at the Bible School. I need to be in Bible School." He enrolled as a full-time student the next term.

When it was time to choose windows, Evangeline did as much research as she could on the subject. She learned that salt water and winter storms cause great damage to windows on the coast. The building was directly above the winter surf line. She needed the window which would best endure the blustery coast conditions.

All of her research pointed to one particular window brand. Naturally, it was also the most expensive on the market. But, if any window would hold up under rugged beach conditions, the Viking would. In an effort to obtain the windows at a reasonable cost, Evangeline tried all of her connections. Nothing turned up.

One morning, Evangeline spent her entire prayer time on the need for windows. It happened to be a couples conference weekend. After the morning session, a man introduced himself to Evangeline as a lumber broker.

"If you need materials," he said, "I may be able to get them for you at considerable savings." Evangeline thanked him warmly. But, lumber she already had. She needed windows.

Some weeks later, Evangeline spoke to the broker

again by phone. Suddenly it occurred to her to ask, "Do you have any contacts for windows?"

"Well, I do," he said, and paused, "but only for one kind of window. I can get a Viking for you."

Lumber, concrete, windows. Evangeline happily, and gratefully received all that God provided. She was also a regular bird dog for bargains. Those around her knew that whenever there was a batch of anything that had little imperfections, Evangeline knew where it was and how to obtain it. When it came time for carpet, she scouted for the best buy. Each supplier was asked, "Haven't you anything for less than that?"

At last a carpet salesman replied, "Well, yes, we have. But it's all red."

"Oh joy," she replied. "That is exactly the color we want."

And so Evangeline came home with red carpet for exactly $1.25 per yard. Though the carpet had some factory imperfections, the men who installed it found they could cut around them quite nicely.

By the Women's World conference of May, 1973 the Beachfront building was nearly finished. Many women had reservations to stay in the new building. Evangeline stayed up most of the night to finish the painting. If women had looked carefully, they would have noticed the paint was still wet when they arrived.

To Evangeline, the building represented tangible evidence of God's faithfulness toward the conference center ministry. Just to look at it, to stand in it's hallway, to view His mighty creation in the ocean breakers below the lounge, made her feel His presence. She sensed His pleasure in providing for His children, in answering their prayer, in meeting their needs. There was an overwhelming sense of praise in Evangeline for this most recent symbol of His abiding presence.

Time and responsibility moved Evangeline forward. The presence of Ecola Hall on campus brought many changes to the winter complexion of the conference center. Perhaps one of the most significant was the return of her daughter, Heather McNeill, to Cannon Beach. Though she was asked to return and help the new Bible School, it was quickly apparent that her mother needed her more than David Duff and Ecola Hall. With everyone's agreement, she became her mother's assistant.

Mother and daughter worked well together. Evangeline had Heather working in many areas. Heather managed the conference center while Evangeline went away on speaking engagements. She supervised the winter guest retreats. She did the daily cash reports. Evangeline freely shared her wisdom and insight into the ministry. She was delighted to train her daughter.

Shortly after the Beachfront was finished, Evangeline received a call from an older woman who lived directly across the city park from the new Beachfront Lodge. She told Evangeline that she needed to talk to her. Would Evangeline and Heather please come for tea the following afternoon?

They were puzzled about this strange request. Though they knew the woman— she was a long time Cannon Beach resident— they had no idea what she could want to talk about. They hoped that their latest project hadn't offended her.

When Evangeline and Heather arrived, they were

relieved to be warmly received. Their neighbor seated them in her parlor. While they enjoyed the ocean view, Mrs. Becker served hot tea and delicious cookies.

She was an elderly woman. A widow. Her husband's family had purchased their oceanfront lots, five of them, at the turn of the century. The first little cottage was built in 1904. Now, the property held three houses. At first, she brought her children to Cannon Beach for summer vacations. They came by buckboard from Portland to Seaside along the Columbia River. Then, they proceeded along the coast to Cannon Beach.

Her husband, a contractor, left her a very wealthy woman. She needed nothing. When at last she came to her point, she spoke slowly and deliberately. "Over the past years, I have been watching your work very carefully. I like you. I like the kind of people you bring to Cannon Beach. Quality people. I like the way you take care of the things you own. You are my kind of people. My children and I have decided to sell this property. We have an offer of $150,000 from one of our neighbors. But, we would like for you to have it. I would be willing to sell to you for $125,000. As I said, we would rather you have it. Please consider my offer, Mrs. McNeill."

Evangeline was flabbergasted. She was as busy as she could be with current projects. She had not considered buying additional property. With care, she explained to the woman about her obligation to pray about the matter. "I wouldn't want to make a mistake," she insisted. "I will give the matter much prayer, and thought."

Heather had been relatively quiet during the whole visit. When they were safely on their way home, she asked her mother, "What do you think?"

178

"I think that until now, I had no plans at all to buy property. But who knows what God may be doing. It certainly is an unusual situation. I'll call all of the board members and ask for their counsel. Then I will do as I explained; I will pray."

The next morning, Evangeline woke with a light heart. When Heather saw her mother, she noticed the lightness in her step. "What have you decided Mother?"

Evangeline explained, "I have decided to offer the woman $80,000."

"But mother, she will be insulted! That isn't what she asked you to consider."

"Well, you may be right. But, we know she has a much better offer. She can always accept that. On the other hand, if she takes our offer, we will know without a doubt that God wants us to have it."

Evangeline arranged to visit the kind woman in her Portland home. It was an elegant, expensive home. She was greeted at the door by a butler. Evangeline carefully explained her offer to Mrs. Becker.

"I hope you don't take offense at our offer. It is just that we had no intention of buying more property. And, in truth, we don't have even $80,000 saved up to pay for this. But, if you accept, I will know that it is God's plan. I will expect him to provide the money as well."

The woman graciously escorted Evangeline to the door. This time it was she who promised to consider the proposition. Only a few weeks later, she told Evangeline that she and her children would be happy to sell her land and buildings to the conference center for $80,000.

Owning this new piece of property enabled Evangeline

to start yet another facet of conference center ministry. In 1974, another young couple approached her with the idea of starting a youth hostel ministry sponsored by the conference center. It would provide Cannon Beach some much needed relief from the young people who traveled freely up and down the coast highway. With little money, they tended to camp in any location— including the beach, local parks and picnic benches in the center of town. The young people were getting to be quite a nuisance to the local businesses.

With the approval of the conference board, Evangeline opened a Youth Hostel right off the beach on the north end of town. The townspeople were delighted to know that Mrs. McNeill would provide a low-cost alternative to public camping. Mrs. McNeill was thrilled that the hostel would expose these young travelers to the gospel. During the first year, the hostel provided housing for over 1,300 youths. Many of these visitors made first time decisions for Christ. Every guest heard the gospel and had an opportunity to respond.

Evangeline's life was filled with more than construction and new ministries. She also had the joy of seeing both her daughters married. On August 7,1971, Helen Jean married Charles Steynor, of Bermuda. Charles, a ruddy complexioned blond, had a charming Bermudian accent. His experience in the hospitality business was an asset to his work at the conference center. Together Charles and Helen Jean presented Evangeline with her first grandchild. Andrew was born December 16,1973.

Evangeline became a devoted grandmother. She always had time for Andrew. She loved to play on the beach and to rough house with the young boy. Perhaps because she was traveling less, she was able to spend much time with him.

Her joy was increased when her oldest daughter, Heather, married Dale Goodenough on May 31,1975. Dale came to the conference center as a student at Ecola Hall. He stayed on working in many capacities. His practical ability with mechanical things made him a much valued addition to the conference family.

The Beachfront lodge was complete. The new property was paid for. Her girls had families of their own. Still, Evangeline's work was not finished. She continued to make plans for the conference center. There was constant repair, upkeep, redecorating. There was always staff coming and going. There were the many students at Ecola Hall. She had discovered the growing opportunity for guest retreats at the conference center during the off-season. More and more weekends found groups of all kinds renting parts of the center to host their private retreats. It was lucrative in that it kept the buildings open, which helped to pay the unrelenting overhead cost. Evangeline, now 71 years old proceeded full steam ahead.

18

The Home Stretch

As the 1976 summer season drew to a close, Heather was growing concerned about her mother's health. While Evangeline participated in all of her usual duties, she seemed to lack her usual zest for life. The staff noticed that her plates often went back to the kitchen untouched. Occasionally, she complained of "stomach problems." After much urging, Evangeline agreed to see a doctor.

The Rinehart Clinic in Wheeler, Oregon, agreed that something was wrong. However, the lab results were not definitive. Mrs. McNeill would need to return for more tests.

Evangeline was convinced that all she needed was rest and sunshine. "I've been asked to speak in Santa Barbara," she reported to Heather. "It will be the perfect 'pick me up.' You'll see. When I return, I'll be my old self."

Heather knew better than to try to convince her mother of anything. Part of her hoped that Evangeline was right. It had been a long conference season. Perhaps extra rest was the solution. At any rate, Evangeline would be traveling with her close friend and companion Faye Southard, and with Rosemary Reed, the conference registrar. Certainly Rosemary, who was a registered nurse, would take good care of mother. Reluctantly, Heather sent Evangeline to California.

Evangeline was gone only a week when the phone call came. It was Faye. Mother was desperately sick. Rosemary believed that she needed to see a doctor. They made arrangements to fly Evangeline to Seattle, where her brother Haldane wanted Evangeline to see his doctor. He would certainly get to the bottom of her illness. Dr. Fred Hutchinson was a very capable specialist.

Evangeline's condition was alarming to Dr. Hutchinson. He admitted her to Swedish Hospital where she underwent several days of testing. Evangeline had a blockage of her colon. She would need surgery.

Walter and Edith came to Seattle to be with Haldane and Ethel and Evangeline. Walter was relieved when he saw Evangeline. Though she was thinner than she had ever been, she was still 'in charge' and had everything under control. The surgery took several hours. The news from Dr. Hutchinson was not good. Evangeline was filled with inoperable cancer.

Nothing prepared Walter for the broken-hearted sister he greeted after surgery. "Walter, it's cancer," she said simply. And she wept. Walter understood her grief. He knew that Evangeline had plans. There was so much to do. So many more things to accomplish. She had no time for illness, much less death. Evangeline had always hoped she would live to see the Lord's return.

In a few days, the old Evangeline was back in control. Together the brothers visited her in the hospital. They went for long walks along hospital corridors. They spent hours planning strategies for her recovery. She was discharged to Haldane's home where she spent another week. Then, just before Thanksgiving, she went to Walter's home in Dallas, Oregon.

The fall weather was unseasonably warm. Evangeline was able to sit for long hours in a sheltered corner of the yard absorbing sunshine and fresh air. As her strength returned, she began to take walks. She planned her trips into town so that she could rest on park benches, and stop at the fabric store and rest at pattern counters. Then she would make the long, slow trek back to Walter's home. Religiously, she followed the treatment and diet prescribed for her. The color returned to her cheeks. She began to gain weight. Life began to feel good again. Hope arose in their hearts. Perhaps she would defeat this evil disease.

While she recovered, her children worked furiously to keep the conference center going. Every week, Heather drove to visit her mother. During their long talks, Heather received her mother's instructions for the staff. Evangeline continued to worry over conference center details.

In her busy lifetime, Evangeline never sat. So, she had not yet discovered the joy of television. But, during her recovery, everyone was surprised at how much she enjoyed Masterpiece Theatre. It was so British. There sat Evangeline, snuggled under a blanket in Walter's recliner, listening to "Upstairs Downstairs."

But not all of her convalescence was spent in resting. The conference center was always on her mind. As soon as she was able, she directed the center by telephone. Walter would find her in the kitchen nearly every morning, impeccably dressed, making phone calls. She was planning the conference program, contacting musicians and speakers, and making arrangements for the coming season.

Evangeline, being a very private person, requested that the truth about her illness be kept from the public. Walter suspected that she felt some shame in having cancer— especially during the rise of the "faith movement." More likely, he thought, Evangeline simply had no intention of dying. She had little patience with the long condolence letters she received. She fully intended to beat this disease. She could not die. She had too much to do.

Barbara Cole approached her cancer differently. She played the organ at summer conferences for many years. Though young enough to be Evangeline's daughter, the two developed an abiding friendship. Barbara looked to Evangeline with great awe and respect. Evangeline was an example to Barbara of what God could do with a woman who was fully His. Barbara and her husband Jim maintained the conference center's piano and organ . Summer after summer, Barbara and her family came to the beach. That is, until the summer of 1973, when Barbara was struck with cancer. Surgery gave Barbara life. Over the next years, Barbara often testified about how God sustained her during her own brush with death.

Barbara heard about Evangeline's illness from another friend on the conference center staff. She knew Evangeline wanted privacy. Evangeline, the spiritual giant, had set her course. Yet, Barbara wondered, Could I have something important for Evangeline to hear? So, risking their friendship, she decided to write to Evangeline.

When Evangeline received Barbara's letter, she was not happy. Another letter of sympathy, she thought. How surprised she was by its words and sentiment.

"Okay kiddo, so you have cancer," it read. "Well, of course we all want you to live a long and healthy life. We are not ready to give up on you. We love you. But, we do have to remember that God is in this. What is His timing? Really, cancer isn't so bad. God will help you live with it or die with it. He has helped me so far. And I know, with certainty, that He will help you. I want you to know that I understand what you are going through. I know too that you are keeping the facts from others. But, I also know from experience, that if you are willing to share with others and be open, you can receive a lot of comfort and healing from people.

"You know, Evangeline, you have been a blessing in my life. When I had cancer, you were there to encourage and care for me. I can never thank you enough for the many prayers you offered on my behalf. I do thank you. Please, Evangeline, don't deny others the privilege of caring for you—just as you have cared for others."

It was quite a surprise to Barbara when she heard that her letter had made a great deal of difference to Evangeline. Of course, Evangeline thanked her. As a result of Barbara's letter, Evangeline became more willing to risk letting people know of her cancer.

Evangeline suffered little during the daytime, there was minimal pain. But the nights were not so pleasant. She suffered constant nausea. For this, she was often up at night eating small bits of food. Sleep was elusive. Walter often rose with Evangeline at night. Ever her caring brother, he would prepare oatmeal or simply sit with her until the nausea subsided enough to allow sleep.

By Christmas, Evangeline was feeling well enough to wish for family. "If only everyone could be together again," she spoke aloud. "How I would love to have everyone spend Christmas together at my house on the coast." Walter called Olive in California, and Helen in Missouri. Haldane agreed to come from Seattle. They would make her wish come true.

It was a wonderful Christmas in Cannon Beach. Evangeline looked so lovely that it was hard to believe she harbored cancer. They spoke of the old days. They took pictures. They sang. They laughed. Christmas of 1976 was just exactly as she had wished.

Evangeline returned to Dallas with Walter and Edith. Her health continued to improve. Her hopes rose higher still.

One of her greatest joys in those days was her only grandchild, Andrew. Though Helen Jean was expecting another child, the baby was not due until spring. In her weariness, Evangeline loved to have Andrew visit. Often she would lock the door to her room, only to be discovered later crawling about on her hands and knees, playing "horsey" with him. After each visit, loneliness overtook her. Her two children lived in Cannon Beach. Walter's Dallas home was too far away for them to visit often. "If only I knew I wasn't going to make it. I would want to spend my time at home, with my girls and with Andrew," she said.

Her longing grew into a request. Walter and Edith struggled with the decision. Her diet was very strict. Her medicine required constant supervision. How would she care for herself at home? Yet, they understood her desire to be near the people and things that were most comforting to her. Reluctantly, they agreed to take her home to Cannon Beach. It would be a good thing for everyone, they decided. The girls would be spared driving to Dallas in the winter weather. Walter and Edith could take a much needed break and visit some Village missionaries in Arizona and Nevada.

Heather made arrangements for a woman to stay with Evangeline in her home. And Evangeline returned to the coast she loved.

When Walter and Edith returned from their trip three weeks later, they got a call from Evangeline. "I think I'd better come back, " she said weakly. Again they made the trip to Cannon Beach. They were not prepared for the change in Evangeline. She had lost weight. Her strength was gone. Her color was bad. Clearly, she had lost a great deal of ground.

How could this have happened, Walter wondered. After some investigation, he discovered that when she arrived at the coast, Evangeline was not content to rest. As soon as she was home, she threw herself back into her work. She hosted meetings in the chapel, and checked up on every conference department. Methodically she had gone to visit every building—the kitchen, the administrative offices and every guest lodge. It was then that Walter realized—Evangeline was saying good-by.

Walter would not give up. Back in Dallas, he and Edith started her on a new and more vigorous treatment program to win back her remission. They made yet another trip to Seattle to visit her doctor. Sadly, he told them there was nothing left to do.

With this news, Evangeline, for the first time, began to realize that she was nearing her own end. There was a kind of gracious acceptance of things as they were. She was not terribly ill. They were grateful for that.

They returned again to Dallas by plane.

Walter encouraged her to complete whatever things she felt she needed to finish. "I think we need to tell the story of the conference center, " she said. "People need to know what has happened there. God has done such wonderful, such impossible things. I want to tell them about it before I go."

With that she began to write. On the back of church bulletins, on old calendars, on scratch paper, Evangeline began to write. It gave her great pleasure.

Helen came from Stonecroft to stay with her at Walter's. Olive came from California, and Haldane from Seattle. The five siblings spent hours together in her room, reading her scratchings and reminiscing about the 'old days.' Together they recreated the details of their lives together— so interconnected, so related. Again Evangeline would rewrite the latest version of her story, and together they would critique the work. They were wonderful hours, precious hours. The Duff evangelistic team was together again.

The doctor in Dallas came to see her once. She refused to go to the hospital. She wanted to be home with her family. They rented a hospital bed. The stream of family and friends coming to visit was a great joy to her.

She delighted in one last precious gift. On May 11, 1977, her second grandchild, Erica, was born. Helen Jean often came to visit with the two children. Mary Rice, her dear friend, brought lamb for Walter's freezer every time she came. Lamb was one food Evangeline was allowed to eat. It was Mary's way of loving Evangeline. She always brought lamb.

As her strength began its final ebb, Evangeline made her last and most important request. During a visit from Heather and Dale she asked the others to leave the room. She began to speak from her heart.

"I am not going to last much longer," she began...

"Mother, please don't talk this way," Heather interjected, and began to cry.

"I must," she insisted. "I love you Heather, you know that. And Dale, I feel as though you are my own son. I wouldn't speak this way unless it was very important to me. I want for you to take over the conference center. I trust you. I know you both understand the dream. I know that together you can guide it, shape it— but not destroy it. It is so important that this is settled before I die. Please. Promise that you will do this for me?"

With many tears, Heather and Dale promised. It was their last visit with Evangeline.

Evangeline slipped into death gently. In the presence of Walter and Helen, on June 16, 1977 at 11 a.m., she flew away. And Archie welcomed her home.

Epilogue

It is morning at the beach. And as I struggle to push away the sleepiness that envelopes me, I dress quickly, careful not to wake the children. Sneaking outside, I find the air is clear and fresh. Even in August, it is chilly this early. I zip up my jacket and pull the collar around my neck. It is foggy, but there is a striking brightness to the day. Experience assures me that the sun will burn through before the morning is over. It feels as though the fog could be swept away by a wave of some massive invisible hand, if only such a hand were available.

I reach the beach quickly and stop to wonder again at its breathtaking beauty. The wheat-colored sand spreads out in every direction. Here the beach is both very deep and miles long. There is a sleepy little creek that winds its way across the beach toward the ocean, almost as though it is in no hurry lose its identity in the sea. To the north a granite point roughly juts out into the water. In the distance, even in the fog, the old lighthouse holds its usual position on the rocks. To the south, one can cross the wide span of sand and arrive at the edge of the creek.

From there it is a comfortable walk on hard sand to "the rock." Here, in Cannon Beach, Oregon, "the rock refers to Haystack Rock, an enormous basalt sentry standing guard at the southernmost end of the village beach. A sanctuary for nesting birds, it is the largest monolith on the coast of the continental United States. At its base, enormous tidepools host a great variety of coastal sealife. Low tides find crowds of families poking and pointing to protected anemones, starfish and crabs.

On this particular morning, I pause to listen again to the sound of the ocean. It is not the mellow lapping of a pond — or even the crash of singular waves. But rather, it is the sound of the waves coming from every direction, melting together in a great symphony of sound. It is an almost deafening sound at this close range. One must speak above the roar. And even then, when you leave, you can still hear it.

For those of us who love this beach, it is a sound that can be called back at any time. It is stored forever, along with the feel of the wind, the sound of the gulls and the smell of the tide. Always in my memory is the unending noise of the ocean.

This memory is so strong that it draws me back, as it has this morning. Again and again I return to experience the magnificence and the power of the setting. Back again to experience the newness of it. Back again to watch the personality of the ocean change with the seasons and the weather.

It is only 7:30 A.M. and the beach is busy with people. Like ants in their divinely directed path, these visitors seem to be making a pilgrimage. They begin at the whale park on the north end of the village, cross the beach and head for "the rock" to the south. Some are young couples, holding hands, deep in conversation. Others protect their white "hairdos" from beach winds with tell-tale chiffon scarves. Some are pairs of women. Some are couples long used to pacing each other on their morning trek to the rock. Sometimes a parent accompanies a child or two, and often on the way back the youngest holds the honored position on top of daddy's shoulders.

An uninformed observer would wonder, as we do with ants, where all these people come from. He would ponder the exactness of the path, and the meaning of the timing. But I have no questions, I know because I share their secret.

It is the secret of this place. Not just the majesty of the north Pacific Coast of Oregon, though that is majesty enough. But it is something even more special, more magnificent, more powerful. Here in this tiny town resides Cannon Beach Christian Conference Center. It is has, for fifty years, been the location of numerous spring and fall weekend and weeklong summer conferences. It is the location of an entire winter full of individual church retreat programs. Here is a place where there is a hole in the heavens. And through the hole, the God who created this grandeur pours himself out to His people. Here, He speaks. Here, He comforts. Here, He heals, restores and refreshes. That is the secret. That is why all these people, families, couples and singles of every age and circumstance flock to this place. To this heavenly outpouring. To this speaking, comforting, healing, restoring, refreshing Father.

The story of this place began years ago. It is the story of a couple, a couple devoted to one another, devoted to their God. It is also the story of one woman's conviction.

195

For 25 years, Evangeline McNeill managed the Cannon Beach Christian Conference Center alone. During this time, she directed nine major building projects, innumerable renovations, upgrades and remodeling projects. The staff grew from a handful of volunteers to nearly 40 paid positions during the summer months. The number of conferences increased from four in 1945, to ten summer conferences and 17 conference weekends in 1976. At the time of her death in 1977, the mailing list contained 18,000 names and the private retreat business was beginning to grow.

In Christian ministry, the death of an originator sometimes leads to the death of the ministry itself. Somehow, momentum is lost. Such has not been the case at Cannon Beach Christian Conference Center. When Evangeline McNeill died, she left behind an army of people who continued to care about and carry on the ministry she began.

Heather McNeill Goodenough assumed the position of Conference Director. With the help of her husband, Dale, her sister Helen Jean, and brother-in-law Charles Steynor, the Conference Center made it through the difficult loss of Evangeline. Heather gave her own unique qualities of leadership to the job. Heather had watched as the enormous growth of the 60s and 70s forced her mother to focus largely on the development of facilities. Evangeline had not had time to develop an administrative structure to support the enormous growth. She had no budget. There were no clearly outlined policies and procedures to manage the conference center staff. There was no regular communication with those who attended the Conference Center. These administrative, "behind the scenes" needs were the ones that Heather strove to meet. Though she was more uncomfortable than her mother speaking in front of groups, she developed the skill to direct a conference session. People who attended the Conference Center during Heather's season as director did not observe much in the way of change, but much was happening to support the Center's extensive growth.

Through the counsel of a fellow Christian conference leader, a Business Manager was hired in 1977. Chuck Davenport and his successor Joe Noegel did much to bring administrative and financial order to a ministry that was growing 10-20% a year through the decade of the 80s, and had been run for 25 years out of one woman's head!

In 1982, Heather hired Janet Kerns to develop a more extensive program for children and families.. Janet wrote a special children's curriculum to replace the vacation Bible school curriculum in use before she came, and added significantly to the activities for families. Janet's organizational talent eventually also moved her into the administration of the guest retreat ministry. On any weekend throughout the winter, there are often three or more private retreats happening on various parts of the campus. Janet and her staff now supervise over 125 private retreats yearly, turning away many more than that due to lack of space.

The following year, a full-time Program Director, Jeff Carlsen, joined the staff to take the programming, advertising and conference M.C.ing load off Heather and help Janet expand the family programs.

When Charles Steynor accepted an administrative job at a conference center in his native Bermuda in 1983, he and Helen Jean left Cannon Beach. His influence at the Conference Center was sorely missed, but Heather continued on as Conference director, aided by a now solid administrative team.

By 1987, Heather was beginning to feel overwhelmed with directing what had become one of the major Christian ministries in the Northwest. Trained as an elementary school teacher, she saw the need to turn the conference operation over to an experienced ministry leader. In 1988, the Board of Directors hired Bob Stephens to become the Cannon Beach Christian Conference Center's fourth Executive Director and first non-family member director.

Bob and his wife, Doris, had been Navigator staff members for 37 years, directing works in Boston England, California, and Colorado. He was General Manager of Glen Eyrie Conference Center in Colorado Springs, Colorado, before coming to Cannon Beach.

Bob's immediate goals included strengthening and stabilizing the Conference Center's financial base, building a stronger ministry to staff and developing a Master Plan of Ministry. Since then, he has overseen the completion of the New Tides building, remodeling of the 43-year-old Kitchen/Dining Room, a renovation of Conference guest facilities and the construction of the new Pacific View oceanfront lodge. Heather chose this time to remove herself from conference administration, focusing instead on Board leadership and developing guest relations.

Not only has there been new growth in facilities, there has also been a new generation of people who have come to love and commit themselves to the ministry of Cannon Beach Christian Conference Center. This new generation never knew Evangeline and Archie

McNeill. Most don't know that Heather is the daughter of the couple who committed their lives to see the Conference Center into existence. Even though these people are not connected with the past generation, they are blessed by the ministry of God which continues day in and day out, year after year in the little resort town of Cannon Beach.